Poverty: A New Perspective

Poverty:
A New Perspective

George L. Wilber,
Editor

The University Press of Kentucky

ISBN: 0-8131-1321-0

Library of Congress Catalog Card Number: 74-7884

Copyright © 1975 by The University Press of Kentucky

A statewide cooperative scholarly publishing agency
serving Berea College, Centre College of Kentucky,
Eastern Kentucky University, Georgetown College,
Kentucky Historical Society, Kentucky State University,
Morehead State University, Murray State University,
Northern Kentucky State College, Transylvania University,
University of Kentucky, University of Louisville, and
Western Kentucky University.

Editorial and Sales Offices: Lexington, Kentucky 40506

Contents

Preface

The main purpose of this book is to provide a foundation for a long-term program of research on poverty. Despite an apparent abundance of information about poverty, problems of poverty persist. Implicit throughout this study is the assumption that we do not know nearly enough about poverty, and that this relative ignorance impedes practical solutions to poverty problems. Considered as a system, poverty is an intricate complexity composed of a multitude of parts. It is this very complexity that is the target in the following pages. Perhaps the task is too big and it is presumptuous for any attacker to hope that answers will come in the near future. At the same time, the dismal failure of past and present efforts to solve poverty problems and the lack of sufficient explanations of poverty constitute a major part of the rationale for a continuing program of poverty research.

From the standpoint of providing social services, interest in research is mainly concerned with results useful for policy and program purposes—results that are helpful in meeting the needs of people more effectively. Research results that lead to instant success in an action program are rare. In fact, solutions to deeply rooted social problems are typically slow and many age-old problems remain unsolved today. Nevertheless, research programs oriented to the solution of real world social problems should help provide answers—ultimately if not immediately.

The initial stimulus and support for this book came from the Social and Rehabilitation Service (SRS), United States Department of Health, Education, and Welfare (Grant numbers 12-P-56016/4-02 and 03). As one of the regional institutes under the SRS program, the Social Welfare Research Institute at the University of Kentucky was assigned the topic of "Poverty in Appalachia." In the process of developing long-range research plans an earlier version of this book, entitled "Anticipating the Poverties of the Poor," was prepared under the auspices of the institute. Concern with research needs and research planning is evident throughout this book.

The topics covered in the following chapters do not exhaust the areas which should receive special attention in research on poverty. Such problems as aging, delinquency and crime, housing, and mental retardation should be subject to intensive examination as components of poverty. Despite the lack of complete and comprehensive coverage of the components of poverty in this book, it was felt that more could be gained from earlier rather than later publication. Future efforts should be devoted to (a) elaboration and refinement of concepts and measures discussed in this book and (b) inclusion of major topic areas not covered here.

The collaboration and cooperation of all contributing authors of this book are apparent in the results. Several other persons also have helped in ways that might be overlooked by those who do not realize that a work of this kind cannot be accomplished without the contributions of many patient, understanding, and talented individuals combining their efforts to reach a goal. Irene Hultman provided excellent editorial service throughout the earlier version of this manuscript. Sandra Burrows, Administrative Assistant, proved invaluable in organizing and directing the multitude of detailed office operations. Rosemary Waters, Karen Conley, Roberta Wilber, Kay Overturf, and Marie Elliott performed the difficult tasks of typing and proofing, for sometimes impatient authors, with admirable diligence and tact.

G. L. Wilber
February, 1974

1 Introduction

George L. Wilber

Why is it that the burdens of poverty must be carried by millions of people in the United States? In the richest, best-educated, most technologically advanced nation in the world—capable of putting men on the moon—little progress has been made toward solving poverty problems. Throughout human history there have always been poor people, and it may be that there is no way in which poverty can be totally eliminated. On the other hand, there is a deep concern over poverty among many who believe that poverty can be drastically reduced. Is it that we do not know enough about the causes and processes of poverty to mount an effective program aimed at its demise? Or is it that we know enough about poverty, but that as a nation we are simply inept at planning, organizing, and manning a program to eliminate poverty? There is no general agreement about why poverty continues to plague the nation.

People in poverty are as much in evidence today as ever. In the minds of many, however, poverty has been relegated to a secondary position, behind such issues as war, population growth, pollution of the environment, and antiestablishment movements. Deprived of its crisis atmosphere, poverty is now a problem area which can be attacked with fewer pressures for instant miracles. Yet at the same time there is also diminished support for the attack on poverty. Millions of impoverished people are as much in need of help as at any time in the past, and some of their needs require urgent and immediate attention. In principle, no one will argue with the precept that direct and effective action should be applied to meet the most pressing needs of the poor. Yet there are deeply rooted dimensions of poverty—not very well understood or recognized—which respond slowly to treatment. Therefore, a major contention in this book is that these fundamental dimensions of poverty—not merely their correlates—need to be recognized and understood. As a basis for an adequate understanding, information and knowledge need to be vastly improved. This understanding then can become a basis for policies and programs to reduce poverty problems. This is not at all a novel idea, but the seriousness and incidence of poverty are such that the remounting of an attack on a long-term basis is certainly in order.

The original impetus for preparing this book was to provide a foundation for research on poverty in Appalachia. It was immediately evident that it might have applicability to poverty research elsewhere. Rather than simply to summarize old ideas, the strategy in the ensuing chapters is to synthesize from them and to develop variations on many of them. Since the concept of poverty is extremely broad, attention is necessarily directed towards specific aspects of poverty. Given the many dimensions of poverty, it remains for future efforts to treat additional facets and to elaborate on those included in this book.

In order to help clarify the perspective of this report, the following assumptions—which some will regard as unwarranted biases—are presented concerning the nature of poverty.

1. *Poverty is a multidimensional object with measurable properties.* A basic notion is that poverty is a system, a construct, possessing multiple properties (Torgerson 1958); these poverty *properties* rather than the system (poverty) are subject to measurement and analysis. It thus becomes necessary to identify the measurable properties or components of poverty.

2. *Most poverty properties represent a continuum.* The customary dichotomy of the poor and nonpoor is an oversimplification that tends to distort reality. Even if we think of poverty as having only one property (e.g., income), we have a continuum. The threshold between dichotomies may be convenient for program purposes, but it is not very useful for purposes of research. Undoubtedly there will be measurement problems when it comes to other poverty properties, but many of these can be resolved.

3. *Poverty properties are geared to the life cycle of individuals and families.* Some poverty properties are evident, or more evident, at

GEORGE L. WILBER

particular age levels. To a large extent, the life cycle is an unalterable process. Some poverty properties, such as a lack of socialization, may be outgrown. Others, such as certain diseases or illnesses, are more likely in old age. The needs for services and assistance also vary with stages in the life cycle. Education and training are paramount needs for relatively young people. Job training and family planning are both relatively important for young adults but irrelevant for the aged.

4. *Poverty properties for individuals and families are not identical to those for communities or regions.* For analytical and program purposes alike, this nonidentity should be clearly recognized. Poverty areas cannot be defined merely by the summation of all the poverty properties of persons within the areas. Neither are the properties of individuals divorced from those of areas in which they live and work.

5. *Determinants of poverty properties include background and intermediate or intervening factors.* Any model designed to explain one or more poverty properties must distinguish causal chains, converging influences, and possibly spurious relationships.

6. *Many poverty properties are essentially processes.* A static, cross-sectional approach cannot yield a comprehensive explanation. As processes continuing over a period of time, poverty properties require explanation through models which incorporate time and change dimensions. Explanation of poverty properties of individuals may require more or less complete life history data. For communities we should have, as a minimum, measures over successive time periods.

7. *Poverty properties and their determinants may be divided roughly into those subject to program manipulation and those which are not.* For program purposes, those properties and determinants which can be manipulated, or manipulated easily, should be identified. Quite obviously such background factors as age or sex cannot be manipulated. Health care, schooling, and job training can be controlled and modified through programs. Suggestions or recommendations for feasible courses of action must necessarily take such distinctions into account. Although this point will not be elaborated in this book, it is critical for action programs.

A major perspective in this book is that poverty is a *system*, an abstraction—unmeasurable by itself—with multiple *properties* which are capable of measurement. The view of poverty as merely lack of income is entirely too simplistic and unrealistic. A conceptual framework for a many-propertied view of poverty is presented in chapter 2. The system of poverty is defined as the relative lack of resources and/or the inability to utilize resources. At a general level, poverty is treated as a function of resources and mobilization. An analytic scheme is suggested whereby the mobilization of resources underlying poverty properties can be handled. Thus, instead of treating poverty as a singular entity which is related to a number of additional characteristics of individuals or regions, factors "related to poverty" are brought into the system.

Since poverty problems persist without benefit of adequate theory or measures, the program-oriented users of research results have had to contend with generally inadequate information. A central thrust of this book is therefore the development of theory-based measures and analysis of poverty which should help increase the knowledge necessary to solve the problems of poverty.

The effort to construct a theory of poverty is not itself a major concern. Rather, an adequate theory of poverty is regarded as a means whereby a poverty research program can move along with a sense of direction. That is, a good theory should: (1) tell us what we need to know and why; (2) help identify the most appropriate variables and suggest measures; and, (3) provide a superstructure within which specific research tasks can be conducted. Thus, one of the functions of this book is to move in the direction of a set of interrelated propositions from which a few at a time can be chosen for empirical testing. This is the strategy for a long-range research program.

The next two chapters focus on the concept and measures of poverty. Chapters 4 and 5 apply the conceptual framework to problems of migration and to the need for services by migrants. In a similar fashion, chapters 6 and 7 examine childbearing as related to the various properties of a poverty system and family planning services as a mechanism for reducing poverty by controlling fertility. Chapters 8 and 9 shift attention to some psychological aspects of poverty. Modernism, internal-external control, and the need for achievement illustrate dimensions of motivation and capability which, if developed, can effectively enhance a person's successful adjustment. A poverty of information resulting from inadequate dissemination of news and information via the mass media and interpersonal communications is the subject of chapter 10. The final chapter returns to problems of theory construction, measurement, and research utilization—threads that run all through the text.

2 Determinants of Poverty

George L. Wilber

Poverty and poverty-related problems plague all modern societies. In recent years a number of expressions have become part of our common jargon—war on poverty, the welfare poor, the medically indigent, ghettos, and so on. Poverty itself is typically regarded as a lack of income, which in turn is related to poor housing, inadequate education, insufficient medical care, excessive fertility, unemployment, and many other depressing problems. Some areas, such as Appalachia, appear as massive concentrations of poverty. According to the Social Security Administration's definition of poverty, the number of poor persons in the United States declined through the 1960s. However, there are indications that, under such programs as Aid to Families with Dependent Children (AFDC), the *incidence* of poverty is on the increase.

Occasionally there are serious efforts to explain why poverty continues; commissions and task forces have studied poverty problems and made recommendations (e.g., the National Advisory Commission on Rural Poverty, 1967). Yet generally there is an atmosphere of "we know all the facts, let's get some action." Much is already known about poverty, but this report takes the position that current knowledge is incomplete and inadequate for the solution of poverty problems. As a result of this lack of knowledge, proposed solutions, plans, and policies and the implementation of public and private programs cannot be totally successful in their objectives of reducing and eliminating poverty.

The major aim in this chapter is to establish a foundation or framework for research on poverty. Despite rather voluminous literature, it is not certain that we yet have an adequate theoretical base for poverty research. There are many broad and sometimes colorful assertions about poverty, but they do not easily yield propositions which can be tested. Ideally what is needed is a system of interrelated propositions from which testable hypotheses may be deduced. The nature of hypothesized relationships between and among variables must be clear and the variables themselves must be capable of measurement.

POVERTY CONCEPTS

Almost everyone understands the meaning of "poverty" but a universally acceptable and unambiguous definition is lacking. In the absence of definitions and measurements, one is restricted to the use of simplistic concepts. For practical purposes it is easy and convenient to use an indicator, like income, as a criterion and to define poverty in terms of those who are below or above some specified threshold, for example, the $3,000 threshold. Once having restricted poverty to those with low incomes, it has been common practice to assemble a multitude of correlates, such as housing, education, employment, health, fertility, mortality, and social participation. Questions of why such factors relate to low income are seldom examined systematically. Even less frequently is there any suggestion that these kinds of factors, also, may be *components* of poverty. Most serious students of poverty are very much aware that a single property (income) is being employed as an indicator and are concerned about the inadequacies of this situation. Thurow (1969:20) expresses the sentiment well when he says, "Depending on usage and aims, there are many relevant definitions of poverty. There is no reason why the definitions should be the same for economic, sociological, or cultural poverty or why the same individuals should be identified under different definitions. There is also no reason why the same definition should be used for every program designed to help the poor."

It may be added that many of us are "hamstrung" by traditional academic backgrounds which condition us to think in terms of economic, sociological, or other relatively narrow perspectives. What does it really matter whether a poverty property is considered part of the realm of some academic discipline? There should be no monopoly on properties included in an analytical model.

GEORGE L. WILBER

Further, many of the commonsense explanations of poverty are not sufficiently articulated or complete to permit reasonable examination with empirical data. The simply stated argument that people are poor because they are lazy illustrates a single-factor explanation which is unlikely to explain much of the variance. The argument that poor people are more likely to suffer ill health illustrates the problem of distinguishing antecedent from consequence. The incidence of high fertility among low income families is common knowledge, but what is known about cause-effect sequences? The main difficulty with such observations and arguments is that first, we are confining our efforts to explaining low income and, second, the arguments are bifactor statements of relationships lacking a clear causal-sequence hypothesis.

Two of the broad attempts to develop an explanation of poverty are represented by the culture of poverty and the cycle of poverty concepts. Both of these concepts consider poverty as something economic; both contribute potentially useful notions about poverty. Neither constitutes an effectively complete theory of poverty.

Oscar Lewis popularized the concept of the culture of poverty. The culture of poverty, he argues, is not merely a matter of deprivation or disorganization, but is something positive with its own rewards. As Lewis (1966:xliv) states, "The culture of poverty is both an adaptation and a reaction of the poor to their marginal position in a class-stratified, highly individuated, capitalistic society. It represents an effort to cope with feelings of hopelessness and despair which develop from the realization of the improbability of achieving success in terms of the values and goals of the larger society." Because of its effect on children, the culture of poverty tends to be self-perpetuating. Moreover, the ones most likely to be influenced are those who come from the lower strata of a rapidly changing society and who are already partially alienated from it. Landless rural workers who migrate to cities, for example, are among likely candidates.

What Lewis calls the culture of poverty is characterized primarily by the low level of integration of and effective participation by the poor in the major activities of society. This absence of participation is explained by such factors as limited economic resources, segregation and discrimination, fear, suspicion, and apathy. Contact of the poor with jails, the army, and public relief is likely to perpetuate the basic poverty as well as the sense of hopelessness. At the local or community level,

Lewis finds poor housing conditions, crowding, gregariousness, and a minimal organization beyond the family. At the family level he notes an absence of a prolonged and protected stage in childhood, early initiation into sex, frequent abandonment of wives and children, a tendency toward mother-centered families, and a strong disposition to authoritarianism. At the individual level he finds a strong feeling of marginality, helplessness, dependence, and inferiority.

As a subculture, the culture of poverty enables some of the poor to adjust. By living for the present, the poor may develop the ability for spontaneity, enjoyment of the sensual, and the indulgence of an impulse. By establishing relatively low levels of aspiration, frustration may be reduced. Violent behavior provides an outlet for hostility and thereby reduces repressions. Lewis estimates that the culture of poverty is limited to about 20 percent of the poor in the United States.

A cycle of poverty, on the other hand, can be defined as a predestination of certain people to a life of (economic) poverty. The idea seems to be that one inherits poverty through his color, his economic status, or the occupation of his parents (Orshansky 1963). As Blau and Duncan (1967) point out, there is little systematic explanation of this concept. There is general agreement that social status is associated with a certain level of income, education, family structure, and community reputation (Lipset and Bendix 1959, among others). These become a part of the vicious circle in which each factor acts on the other to perpetuate the social structure and the individual family's position. The cycle argument holds that disadvantages are cumulative.

Blau and Duncan (1967) disagree in part with the vicious circle argument. First, they ask, how difficult is it for the individual to change his status? Based on national sample data they find a correlation between father and son occupational status of about .40. Evidently a noticeable amount of intergenerational mobility does occur. One might ask, then, how much mobility must occur to offset the notion of a vicious circle? Second, the proposition is set forth that occupational origin is associated with many factors, with each factor operating on the other so as to perpetuate the family's cumulation. However, Blau and Duncan argue that if several determinants (such as father's occupation and education) are substantially intercorrelated, their combined effects are largely redundant.

There are legitimate and meaningful aspects of the notion of a vicious circle of poverty. Analysis of cohorts is one way of examining cumulative effects. In this case what is cumulative is the experience of an individual or group of individuals over the life cycle. Occurrences in the later stages of the life cycle depend on prior achievements. Also, there are some underprivileged groups, especially Negroes, whose background handicaps produce cumulative effects. A Negro's chances of occupational success in the United States are far inferior to those of a white. The effects of being Negro are cumulative, but this is not the case for other groups. The occupational success of southern whites is less than that of northern whites and Negroes, whether the southerner remains in the South or migrates to the North. However, the handicaps of white southerners do not have cumulative effects on their occupational chances (i.e., the inferior background and education of southern whites completely account for their limited occupational chances). Second-generation immigrants are less advantaged than northern whites with native parents, but their occupational achievements are as high as those in the majority group.

Like most concepts of poverty, the culture and the cycles concepts focus on only one dimension. Nevertheless, it is clear that multiple factors are involved. Lewis's work is suggestive of a number of dimensions or properties of poverty. A starting point for examining the nature of poverty, then, is to view poverty as a multidimensional object with measurable properties.

POVERTY PROPERTIES: A CLASSIFICATION

The following discussion attempts to identify some general properties in relation to basic resources and mobilization. A broad system for classification is suggested in which poverty properties are divided for taxonomic reasons into those that relate primarily to (a) the life cycle of an individual and (b) areas, regions, or collectivities of people.

The nature of the life cycle suggests that some poverty properties are more likely to manifest themselves at certain stages than at others. Health problems associated with aging or a reduction in income at retirement, for example, are properties closely connected to the life cycle. Table 2.1 shows a very general and overly simplified scheme for identifying various poverty properties in relation to five basic characteristics or resources of an individual. The ability of a person to utilize these resources effectively will help determine the nature and extent of

TABLE 2.1 Poverty Properties of Individuals

Resources	Mobilization	Poverty properties
Health	Actual use of health facilities and services Personal hygiene	Handicap: physical and/or mental Disease Injury

Capability
  capacities,
  abilities,
  skills
	Education and training facilities and services
	Employment
		Low education and/or training
		
		Unemployed; underemployed
		Low income

Motivation: drives, norms	Goal achievement process	Blocked goals Reduced goals Frustration
"Personality"	Socialization Maturation	Unsocialized Antisocial Social isolation
Socioeconomic status	Status achievement	Low mobility Low status

his poverty. The properties listed in the right-hand column are potentially related to several basic resources in the first column. Low income, for example, may be a function of health and motivation as well as education and skill.

Based on these five resources, there are five general kinds of poverty properties: poverty of (1) health, (2) capability, (3) motivation, (4) personality, and (5) socioeconomic status. The manner and degree to which one is blessed with these resources will influence his probability of relative prosperity. There are possible connections between resources and their mobilization as well as interrelations among basic resources.

Health poverty

The health status of a person at birth and at subsequent points in his life is related to the nature and degree of his physical and mental

GEORGE L. WILBER

handicaps. We use the term "handicap" to refer not only to permanent and total disabilities but also those of a temporary or partial nature, resulting from injuries, diseases, and accidents. A person could be disabled at birth and suffer a lifelong handicap. Many people acquire a handicap of some sort during the course of their lifetime. Some degree of control over personal health and individual handicaps is potentially available in at least two major forms: personal hygiene practice and the use of health facilities and services. The ability to use, or the opportunity to have access to, the health care system constitutes the mobilization of resources for a person. This mobilization may help prevent, cure, or reduce the handicap of the person. Regardless of income and other considerations, a person can suffer a poverty of health.

Capability poverty

The second kind of basic resource possessed by an individual is his capability, part of which he receives through the mechanism of heredity and part of which is socially acquired. To the extent that inherited capacities of an individual are meager, his potential for skill development is restricted; a great part of one's capability is acquired, however, and thus is of primary concern here. If a person is to develop his initial capability, he must go through a learning process. In general this means he must be able to effectively utilize available education and training facilities and services. Several poverty properties may result from underdeveloped abilities and skills. The lack of skill development may lead to unemployment or underemployment. Thus the ability of a person to obtain a job which will provide a reasonable income is a major part of his mobilization ability. If for any reason he cannot develop the necessary skills and obtain an appropriate level of employment, low income or joblessness may result.

Motivational poverty

Forces that drive a person to do whatever he does are an important part of his basic resources. His ability to apply these drives to achieve goals is a primary intervening factor between basic drives and goal achievement. Factors beyond his control may of course block his efforts. In any case if he is unable to achieve goals, he suffers from a motivational or achievement poverty. Discrepancies between goals and achievements indicate a kind of failure. Even if he reduces his goals, which may help to reduce frustration, he suffers from a kind of achievement poverty. One of the very difficult aspects of motivational poverty is the fact that one person may set very modest and realistic goals that are easily attainable, while another shoots for the moon very unrealistically and fails. Who suffers the greater motivational poverty?

Personality poverty

This poverty component is essentially a gap between generally accepted norms and those interiorized and accepted by a person. Within their particular environments some people are relatively unsocialized and others are antisocial. In either case nonconforming behavior may result. Personality is usually considered as primarily learned and would normally include childhood socialization. To the extent that a person fails to acquire accepted social customs and norms, he is an unsocialized nonconformist. However, since socialization is essentially a lifelong process, the degree and nature of socialization does not necessarily remain constant. Some people will effectively interiorize prevailing norms and values, but tend to reject them or rebel against generally accepted goals and/or the means of achieving these goals. These people are nonconformists in this sense even though they may be innovators or inventors. A poverty of socialization may also exist for those who do not participate as extensively in activities and groups as do most people with similar characteristics.

Status poverty

Much of the discussion about poverty centers around class or socio-economic status, or, more specifically, income, occupation, and education. Low social status, however it is measured, is one of the most common designations of poverty. Within the life cycle perspective, a person acquires his status initially from his parents and this ascribed status is a major determinant of his subsequent status. The extent to which a person can effectively achieve a higher status in an "open class" society reflects his ability to apply not only his initial status resources but also his other resources. Regardless of the reasons for achieving or not achieving a higher status, the initial occupancy of a low position in the social hierarchy and the inability over time to attain upward mobility are indicators of poverty.

In the foregoing discussion, a number of properties of the poverty system have been related to the life cycle. Other poverty properties can be placed in the context of communities or regions.

GEORGE L. WILBER

For analytical and program purposes, poverty properties of geographic areas or collectivities of people can be treated separately from those for individuals (Wilber 1972). Basic resources, ability to mobilize these resources, and the resulting poverty properties are somewhat different for geographic areas than for individuals. In reality, of course, the two are closely related. In Table 2.2, seven basic resources are identified as a basis for distinguishing poverty properties: natural resources, state policy, the economic system, social norms, the stratification system, community services and facilities, and the mass media. This listing is not ordered on a priority basis.

Natural resource poverty

In Appalachia, the Ozarks, the desert Southwest, and other areas, there is abundant evidence of either the absence of adequate natural resources, failure to utilize available resources, or depletion and waste of existing resources. Thus, a poverty of natural resources can mean different things depending on specific circumstances. Given a set of natural resources in an area, at least two kinds of activity help determine their usage: technological development and population settlement patterns. Resources may not be used effectively if existing technology is inappropriate for their use or is not applied. Resources may be depleted too quickly and unwisely from the standpoint of the welfare of residents. Historically, settlement patterns have played a major role in the use of natural resources. This is well illustrated in the case of Appalachia where the relative abundance of resources helped attract people to the area, and where now, because of such things as changes in mining technology, reliance on other sources of power, and the absentee owner system, residents of Appalachia live in a vast "poverty area." With the present use of the natural resource base in Appalachia, many residents have a choice of either emigrating in search of more favorable opportunities or of remaining and fighting for economic survival. Hypothetically, a "better use" of existing natural resources could reduce much of the economic poverty of Appalachia.

Policy poverty

Given that there are needs to be met and governments—federal, state, and local—with an obligation to help meet these needs, potentially there is a poverty of state policy. Popularly we speak of the "welfare poor," a group whose needs are met to some extent by one or more

TABLE 2.2   Poverty Properties of Areas & Collectivities of People

Resources	Mobilization	Poverty properties
Natural resources	Technological development and application Settlement patterns	Depletion Waste
State policy	Program goals, coverage, administration funding Legislation Judicial process	Unmet needs "Welfare poor" Ineligibility for benefits
Economic system	Acquisition of property rights Labor and capital Production, distribution and consumption	Inability to acquire or exchange goods or services Lack of ownership or management control High proportions of low income and unemployment High proportions of low living levels
Social norms	Accessibility Acceptability	Norm deprivation Indifference to or rebellion against norms
Stratification	Social mobility, actual and potential	High proportions of nonmobile, low status
Community services and facilities	Use of leadership and organization to reduce poverty problems	Lack of leadership and organization Absence of effective services and facilities
Mass media	Dissemination of news and information	High proportions of uninformed citizenry

GEORGE L. WILBER

governmental programs. We have developed a multiplicity of policies, goals, and programs designed in general to serve the needs and reduce the burdens of people who, it is felt, require help. It is admittedly difficult to define these needs unambiguously and unequivocally so that we can design programs which will close gaps. Yet to the extent that coverage and benefits of specific programs do not serve "those in need," there is an ineffective mobilization of effort. The situation is complicated further by the fact that the legislative structure and judicial processes are relatively slow and often fail to keep pace with changing conditions. For example, in the past, individuals were sometimes ineligible for the benefits of certain programs by virtue of crossing a state line and failing to meet residence requirements; even now such barriers have not been completely eliminated. In a highly mobile society, residence requirements are questionable standards for eligibility. There is a need for policies designed to alleviate problems of this sort.

Economic poverty

The economic system and all that it includes constitute a basic resource. The ability of a nation, region, or community to mobilize its economic resources is a major determinant of many of the properties of poverty. The way in which the economic system is structured to control or facilitate the acquisition of property rights, for example, is one of the important ways in which a population's access to housing and consumer goods is controlled. Labor and capital may be considered basic resources, but they exist within the context of the economic system. Their nature and the extent to which they can be effectively mobilized are obvious and instrumental determinants of what might be termed economic poverty. Mobilization of the means of production, distribution, and consumption are equally vital to the economic welfare of a population.

When mobilization of economic resources somehow fails, one or more properties of economic poverty are likely to characterize an area's population. There are too many specific properties of economic poverty to enumerate, but Table 2.2 suggests several possibilities. A relative inability to exercise the rights of ownership or management control illustrates one of these. The inability of people as consumers to acquire or exchange goods and services may be largely a function of their personal income but it may also be a function of a faulty distribution system. Where high proportions of the population manifest low levels of living, opportunities for the acquisition of property rights are likely to be restricted in some way. Then, of course, there are the customary indicators of poverty: high proportions of low income and unemployed persons.

Norm poverty

As a result of isolation and traditions, people in some areas and communities are unable or unwilling to accept prevailing social norms which, as standards of behavior, help guide people's actions. As Oscar Lewis (1966) and others have pointed out, subcultures exist in which the norms differ from those in the larger society. In many communities local norms are not entirely consistent with those found elsewhere. There are well-known difficulties in identifying social norms but this does not negate their importance as a basic resource. Lewis provides an ample number of illustrations of people in economic poverty who not only are able to adjust to their circumstances by developing a culture of poverty but in many cases are hindered from moving out of economic poverty by adherence to their own set of behavior standards. When the mobilization of generally accepted norms is discussed, the accessibility and acceptability of these norms are among the primary considerations. When they are essentially inaccessible, norm deprivation results; when unacceptable, either indifference or rebellion against the prevailing standards occurs. It is acknowledged that norm poverty properties are measurable, although in general no great success in this area has been achieved.

Social class poverty

Poverty in many ways is equated with low social class. The concern here, however, is with the system of stratification itself as a kind of basic community resource, the extent to which the system permits and facilitates upward mobility, and the resulting numbers and proportions of people occupying low status. Social hierarchies, by definition, contain occupants of relatively low status, but some hierarchical systems are more flexible than others in allowing for mobility. While an extended discussion of social stratification and mobility is beyond the scope of this study, we can stress the point that the presence of high proportions of nonmobile, low status persons who are somehow unable to achieve higher status represents a poverty property. By making

GEORGE L. WILBER

available opportunities in education, employment, housing, and other areas, a society or community can facilitate upward mobility. The extent to which upward mobility is realized is a critical aspect of poverty.

Facility and service poverty

Community facilities and services are increasingly an important part of basic resources. The quality, quantity, and availability of such resources represent the ability of a community to mobilize itself to meet the needs and desires of its people. For those who suffer from economic or health poverty, the ability of community leadership and organization is a matter of primary importance. Limited facilities and services and a lack of effective leadership and organization reflect a service-facility poverty.

Mass media poverty

Cutting across most of the other poverty properties is a poverty of mass media. It is not that the media themselves are so important, but that the media are instrumental in dissemination of news and information. In communities where few have access to information, an uninformed citizenry is bound to result. Perhaps this should be called a poverty of information and certainly it is closely akin to the acquisition of knowledge and skills.

A number of relatively small and isolated communities in rural areas lack daily newspapers and radio and television coverage. In the more mountainous parts of Appalachia, reception over the air waves is either difficult or impossible. Local weekly papers generally confine their contents to information of a local nature. It may be doubted that many would read metropolitan papers or national magazines even if they were easily available. But whatever the reasons and circumstances, when large numbers of people are uninformed about matters that can and do affect their welfare, this is as much a kind of poverty as the lack of income.

In sum, the identification of the properties of poverty on the basis of total resources, together with the nature and degree of mobilization, provide a broad framework for the analysis of poverty. The classifications proposed in Tables 2.1 and 2.2 are by no means final, and for that matter, not even immediately useful for research purposes. With this kind of framework, however, one can begin to develop fairly specific notions about determinants of poverty. For analytical purposes there is a semblance of neatness in dividing poverty as an object into its properties, each of which is in some degree measurable. The life cycle of individuals provides a convenient basis for separating properties primarily attributed to individuals. The recognition of communities or regions helps distinguish properties more nearly related to collectivities of people than to individuals. The fact that families and individuals actually live in communities means that we capture only a part of reality with this kind of abstraction.

The next step is to explore briefly how we might formulate testable propositions—statements of the dependency of one or more poverty properties on resources and their mobilization.

POVERTY PROPERTIES AS FUNCTIONS OF RESOURCES AND MOBILIZATION

In order to examine systematically the contribution of determinants of poverty properties, one or more analytical models must be developed and employed with specific empirical data. The tentative classifications in Tables 2.1 and 2.2 constitute a meager beginning at best, but they can be used to formulate a general model from which specific variations can be developed. Propositions relating one or more determinants to one or more poverty properties can be verbalized and also stated in the form of concise equations. Yet there are few ready-made testable propositions in the literature on poverty. The following discussion is based largely on the work of Blalock (1967) in which he was concerned with the development of a theory of minority group relations. Those familiar with his work will note similarities to the strategy suggested here.

We can take an initial position that poverty is largely a function of two general types of variables: the degree of availability of total resources and mobilization. The actual source of poverty is the relative lack of resources. For individuals, the source is the lack of those properties that provide the power potential or the ability to exercise power (Blalock 1967:113). For communities or regions, sources of poverty are the paucity of resources of the area and its inhabitants, or the properties which provide the ability to exercise influence to accomplish goals. Mobilization refers to the proportion of total resources actually used or expended to achieve a given objective.

GEORGE L. WILBER

A general proposition can be expressed very simply. A poverty property is a function of resources and mobilization. Q can represent a continuum of wealth or prosperity ranging from zero to 1.0. If the function is multiplicative, we can say that specific poverty property, P_i, is a function of resources, R, and mobilization, M. Thus we have

$$Q_i = 1 - P_i = RM \qquad (1)$$

According to this statement, the interaction between resources and mobilization determines the degree of a specified kind of poverty. If poverty is defined as the actual overcoming of resistance within a standard period of time, several potentially important influences are ignored, including motives, goals, and the means of exercising power. Therefore beginning with equation (1), additional factors must be introduced in the development of a more comprehensive statement. One of the grounds for uncertainty in elaborating equation (1) is a question of whether determinants included on the right hand side of the equation are related in an additive or in a multiplicative fashion. At the moment, there is no basis for making this decision.

The basic equation can be varied and expanded in a variety of ways. A few of these can be illustrated. If a poverty property is treated as proportional to resources times mobilization, we have

$$Q_i = k_i RM \qquad (2)$$

where k_i is a factor of proportionality. As components of mobilization we can introduce motive strength, m, expectancies of achieving objectives, E, and incentives, I(i.e., rewards or punishments). If mobilization is taken as proportional to motive strength, expectancy, and incentive values, we have

$$M = k_2 mEI \qquad (3)$$

where k_2 is a proportionality factor. That is, in equation (3), mobilization is a function of motivation, expectancies, and incentives for achieving a specific goal. Expectancy can be defined as proportional to resources.

$$E = k_3 R \qquad (4)$$

In equation (4), the expectation of achieving a goal is dependent on resources. Finally, combining equations (2), (3) and (4) into a single statement, and ignoring error terms, we have

$$Q_i = k_i (mI) R^2 \qquad (5)$$

This equation relates a poverty property to resources and a motivational component, (mI), but excludes expectancies. These equations are far short of a complete theory, but they serve to illustrate how a general proposition can be varied to include more specific and additional factors.

We can illustrate the use of the general model as a means of examining a specific hypothetical problem. Suppose we want to explain the income a person received during the previous year. We might argue that his income is directly dependent on his occupation, age, and color—that is, his resources—and on his motivations, expectancies, and incentives for earning income. As background factors, age and color are surrogates for other factors that might be determinants of income. Occupational level can be scored on at least an ordinal scale (Blau and Duncan 1967). Scales can be developed for measuring the mobilization factors of motivations, expectancies, and incentives. An ordinary linear regression equation can be used to state concisely the nature of the expected relationships.

$$Y = a + b_1 X_1 + b_2 X_2 + \ldots + b_k X_k \tag{6}$$

We can denote the variables in the following manner. Let:

Y: annual income
a: a constant
b_i: a weight attached to variable i (i=1,2, . . . , k)
X_1: occupational level
X_2: age
X_3: color
X_4: motivation
X_5: income expectancy
X_6: income incentive

Ignoring error terms and interactions, a complete statement of the dependency of annual income on these resources and their mobilization is

$$Y = a + b_1 X_1 + b_2 X_2 + b_3 X_3 + b_4 X_4 + b_5 X_5 + b_6 X_6 \tag{6a}$$

Despite the neatness of this proposition, it may or may not be adequate to explain income. Some important determinants have undoubtedly been left out.

A similar strategy can be used to explain poverty properties of communities. Suppose we want to explain the poverty property of social mobility in a community. We can define mobility as movement between a man's first job and his present or last job. For the labor force in the community, the proportion of persons who are nonmobile is an indicator of poverty of mobility. A low degree of mobility could be attributed to high proportions of Negroes, high proportions of adults

　　　　　　　　　　　　　　GEORGE L. WILBER

with less than high school education, relatively few who have had any job training within the previous ten years, and a general absence of norms and aspirations for upward mobility.

A linear regression equation similar to equation (6a) can be written with the appropriate notational system for the variables. Data necessary to determine the fit of the model could be obtained through a field survey. Essentially this model would attempt to explain the prevalence of social mobility (i.e., job mobility) on the basis of selected factors. In contrast to the previous illustration, in this instance aggregate data are used.

From Table 2.2, it is evident that measures or indicators for the mobilization and resource variables can be very difficult to obtain. How does one measure state policy, the economic system, or the stratification system? How does one identify and measure the degree of disorganization in community services and facilities? How does one determine accessibility to social norms, and which norms should be considered? These are not insoluble problems, but such questions suggest that much work remains to be done.

Recent work in the area of social indicators is aimed at producing measures which, along with policy and program utilities, can become very useful for analytical purposes. Preceded by the development of economic indicators, social indicators have acquired a variety of connotations—social accounts, bookkeeping, intelligence, reporting, and monitoring. Land (1971) argues that, in order to be useful, indicators must satisfy three criteria: they must be components of a social system model; they must be collected and analyzed at various times and accumulated into time series; and they must be aggregated or disaggregated to levels appropriate to the specifications of the model.

While the ultimate accomplishment of the indicator movement is a matter for speculation at this time, one can expect a gradual improvement and expansion of the data base which will be used increasingly to provide measures of specific conditions and trends. Depending to a great extent on the quality of indicators and how well they meet Land's criteria, more adequate indicators of the kind required by a resource-mobilization model can be expected.

Readers will quickly recognize many possible alternatives in a general analytical model, both in the way in which it is formulated and elaborated and in the variety of statistical and analytical techniques employed to yield answers. Part of the task for the future is to develop specific and possibly competing models and to test a given model with various analytical techniques in different populations at different times. Gradually it should be possible not only to identify major determinants of poverty properties but to generalize at broader levels.

CONCLUDING COMMENT

This chapter has attempted to sketch a framework for poverty research. The general perspective has been interdisciplinary, theoretical, and methodological on the grounds that neither scientific nor program advances can be accomplished effectively without this kind of perspective. Thus far, scientific and mission-oriented accomplishments under the heading of poverty have been modest at best. One would be hard pressed to argue steadfastly that we really know and understand much about poverty or that we, as a society, have moved adequately and successfully toward its reduction and elimination.

The word *poverty* itself has become an obstacle. For scientific research purposes, poverty is like many ordinary words. It lacks the sharpness and precision required of scientific concepts. It often carries emotional connotations. It is partly for these reasons that there has not been an acceptable theory of poverty, despite the great abundance of verbiage. For policy and program purposes, poverty has been both a slogan and a term employed to define and delimit agency jurisdictions. The "war on poverty" was to eliminate poverty. Much of the federal eradication effort was centered in a single agency, although clearly other agencies were concerned and active. As a result, area or community development, slum clearance, family planning, job training, rehabilitation, and many other programs were supposedly divorced from the war on poverty.

Thus it might be argued that "poverty" should be abandoned in favor of some more suitable term for scientific reasons. A neutral and abstract "Y" could serve the purpose nicely, but who ever heard of a "war on Y" or rising above the "Y-Line." For political purposes "Y" has no zing. Poverty or some fashionable and attractive synonym is likely to persist for political and governmental purposes.

Levity aside, it is far more important in developing a program of research to set forth significant objectives, to specify the component parts of a system, and to direct analysis toward cause-effect relationships than to spend much time worrying about the label. This is why

GEORGE L. WILBER

poverty continues to be the identifying designation throughout this book.

The fact remains, whether we call it poverty or "Y" the object of attention is an abstraction. From the standpoint of measurement theory, poverty is viewed here as a construct, a system of objects and things. The observables in the real world are *properties*, and, once defined, properties *of* something—that is, the system. Although the distinction between systems and properties is perhaps obvious, it is an extremely important one. In the present context, it is always the properties that are measured and not the system.

3 Poverty Measures as Indicators of Social Welfare

J. Patrick Madden

It is not to die, or even to die of hunger that makes a man wretched; many men have died; all men must die. . . . But it is to live miserable and know not why; to work sore and yet gain nothing; to be heart-worn weary, yet isolated, unrelated, girt in with a cold universal Laissez-faire.

Thomas Carlyle

In 1960 nearly one in every four persons was poor, compared with one in eight in 1970. The absolute number of poor persons, 40 million in 1960, declined each year until 1969, which had the lowest number of poor persons ever reported in recent history—24.1 million. The biggest reductions occurred during the rapid economic expansion of the mid-1960s, as unemployment dropped from more than 6 percent to less than 4 percent (Figure 3.1). Then in 1970, as the economy slid into a recession, unemployment increased from 3.5 to 4.9 percent and the downward trend in the number of poor persons was reversed. Of course, the poverty trends are subject to a wide range of social, economic, and political variables, including the possibility of a modified income maintenance system. Nonetheless, with unemployment hovering around 5 to 6 percent, the number of persons in poverty has remained above 24 million.

What do these trends imply with regard to social welfare? Is a downward trend in the number of persons officially counted as "poor" a sure sign of a better life?

The purpose of this chapter is to examine the poverty statistics and trends in detail, placing the underlying concepts into a framework that will reveal their relevance and validity as indicators of trends in general well-being. Deprivation is examined in terms of a number of dimensions, with emphasis on income, adequate food, health, and longevity.

Two basic criteria are used to guide the inquiry into poverty statistics: *Criterion 1:* accuracy of the poverty data for a given year in representing the degree of perceived deprivation in that year. *Criterion 2:* adequacy of the trends in poverty data in reflecting the changes in the social welfare over time.

THE MEANING OF POVERTY

In his assumptions regarding the nature of poverty, Wilber (chap. 1) has articulated an idealized and highly meaningful concept of poverty. Much less ideal is the official United States government definition of poverty (or "low income" as it is currently called by the Census Bureau).

The official definition ignores the multidimensional nature of poverty; it is based strictly on family income during a single year; it largely ignores the family life cycle as a process affecting deprivation. Nonetheless, it is widely used as an eligibility criterion for public programs, and it is the basis for the proliferating tabulations of poverty data from the decennial census, the annual Current Population Survey conducted by the Census Bureau, and countless smaller scale surveys made by researchers throughout the nation.

Poverty is officially defined in terms of the adequacy of current family income to meet a constant, absolute standard of consumption, based on family size and farm versus nonfarm residence. Table 3.1 indicates the poverty line—poverty thresholds for various sizes of family—as of 1970. The amounts of income indicated by the poverty line vary not only with size of family and farm versus nonfarm residence, but also, to a lesser degree, with the sex and age of the head of the household.

In saying that 24 million people are "poor," as defined by the federal poverty statisticians, what do we really mean? We are counting the number of persons in households with incomes below the levels shown in Table 3.1. Clearly poverty means much more than low income. Income is only a part of socioeconomic status, which in turn is only one of five poverty properties listed by Wilber in chapter 1.

Another study lists six broad dimensions of poverty: (1) income, (2) assets or wealth, (3) access to basic services (e.g., health, transportation, legal services), (4) social mobility and education, (5) political power, and (6) status and satisfaction (S. M. Miller et al. 1967). Each of these general dimensions of poverty include a number of aspects, all of which tend to be highly correlated and causally related. For example, where poverty is widespread the quantity and quality of social services is usually poor—a consequence of the economic imperative that in a market economy, demand creates its own supply. Demand in this sense is not merely need. Rather, demand is a function of purchasing power, and purchasing power is not congruent with need. Thus, low income can lead to lack of access to social services, in terms both of availability and of ability to pay. Publicly supported social services and income transfers in kind (e.g., Medicare and Medicaid) represent efforts to bypass and supplement the market economy, thereby tending to break the link between these two dimensions of poverty—low income and lack of access to social services.

More will be said later about the nonincome dimensions of poverty. First, the income aspect will be examined.

THE PREMISES UNDERLYING
THE OFFICIAL POVERTY DEFINITION

Poverty lines are calculated each year for various sizes of family and for farm-nonfarm residence, based on a constant "subsistence" level of consumption expenditure. Four major premises underlie the calculation of these official poverty lines:

1. The first premise establishes the general income level of the poverty line. In the base year, 1963, a family of a given size at the poverty line has enough income to afford the USDA economy food plan for that size of family. The economy food plan is based on a rather frugal menu, designed to provide a skilled homemaker enough food to feed her family adequately for a short time, or in emergency situations.

2. A family at this subsistence level will spend one-third of its income on food. This, in conjunction with the first premise, implies that the base-year poverty line is three times the economy food budget.

J. PATRICK MADDEN

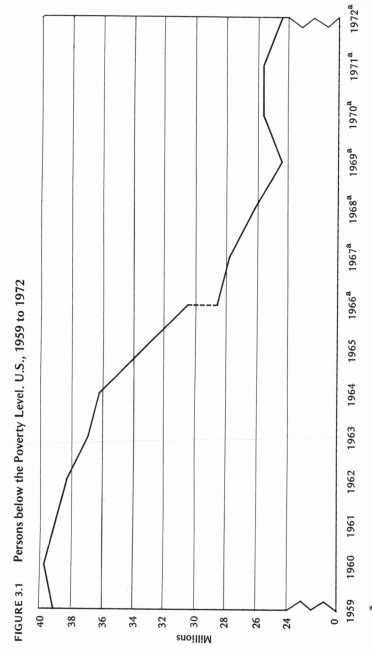

FIGURE 3.1   Persons below the Poverty Level. U.S., 1959 to 1972

aBased on revised methodology (U.S., Bureau of Census 1973)

3. Farm families are assumed to need only 85 percent as much income as nonfarm families of the same size.

4. Starting with the 1963 base year, annual adjustments in purchasing power of the poverty thresholds may be represented by changes in the Consumer Price Index (CPI) (U.S. Bureau of Census 1969).

The least controversial premises will be examined first, working from the fourth to the first.

A key question in the selection of a method for making yearly adjustments in the poverty line is the matter of the representative "poverty market basket." Do the prices of the things purchased by the poor go up at the same rate as the items represented in the CPI? Hollister's analysis (1969) of expenditure patterns of a sample of poor households suggests there is very little difference between the CPI and a "poor people's CPI."

However, in view of the wide range in price levels and cost-of-living in various parts of the nation, it is clear that the "poverty line" level of income will buy considerably less in some locations than in others. If the procedure were changed to include some locational differentials in the CPI, the poverty lines would reflect more nearly the same level of real income or purchasing power in different places.

Thus, the price adjustment feature of the poverty threshold definition is somewhat deficient in regard to Criterion 1—it may, by failing to reflect a constant purchasing power in all locations, introduce some distortion into the national picture of deprivation in any one year. However, because the locational price differentials tend to be rather stable, this feature probably does not significantly distort the trends over time and thus meets Criterion 2.

At the poverty line, farm families are assumed to need only 85 percent as much income as nonfarm families to be at the equivalent level of living. This farm-nonfarm ratio was first increased from its original level of 60 percent to 70 percent. In an attempt to reexamine this ratio (Madden et al. 1968), the authors adhered (for purposes of comparability) to the first and second premises of the official poverty lines. Using multiple regression analysis of family expenditure data, their study derived the farm-nonfarm ratio of approximately .85. This ratio was subsequently adopted by the Census Bureau as official, the decision being based on this and other studies reviewed by an interdepartmental task force. Further analysis by Carlin and this author (1971), employing the same basic assumptions and data from the

J. PATRICK MADDEN

TABLE 3.1 Weighted Average Thresholds at the Poverty Level in 1972

Size of family	Total	Nonfarm			Farm		
		Total	Male head[a]	Female head[a]	Total	Male head[a]	Female head[a]
All unrelated individuals	$2,101	$2,109	$2,207	$2,046	$1,774	$1,824	$1,723
Under 65 years	2,163	2,168	2,254	2,085	1,861	1,916	1,772
65 years and over	1,994	2,005	2,025	2,000	1,708	1,722	1,698
All families	3,788	3,813	3,854	3,524	3,277	3,287	3,072
2 persons	2,703	2,724	2,734	2,670	2,296	2,302	2,197
Head under 65 years	2,790	2,808	2,823	2,729	2,393	2,399	2,258
Head 65 years and over	2,505	2,430	2,532	2,516	2,153	2,154	2,141
3 persons	3,319	3,339	3,356	3,234	2,830	2,838	2,702
4 persons	4,247	4,275	4,277	4,254	3,643	3,644	3,598
5 persons	5,011	5,044	5,048	4,994	4,302	4,301	4,355
6 persons	5,633	5,673	5,679	5,617	4,851	4,849	4,900
7 or more persons	6,917	6,983	7,000	6,841	5,947	5,963	5,771

Source: U.S., Bureau of the Census, Current Population Reports, Series P-60, No. 91, "Characteristics of the Low Income Population: 1972," Government Printing Office, Washington, D.C., Dec. 1973.

[a]For unrelated individuals, sex of the individual

1960-61 Survey of Consumer Expenditures but using a considerably more refined analytical model, resulted in the same basic conclusion. That is, the farm-nonfarm ratio of .85 seems to reflect equivalent levels of living for certain broad aggregates of farm and nonfarm families. However, the ratio was found to vary widely from one kind of urbanization to another, and with family size, as shown in Table 3.2.

This variation, of course, is not surprising. But neither is it definitive. For example, the ratio for central cities of Standard Metropolitan Statistical Areas (SMSAs) was about .85 for a four-person family, but the ratio seems to decline with larger families. This relationship would, at face value, indicate it may be relatively less expensive to rear larger families on a farm than in an urban location. However, this result must not be taken as definitive, as the method used for this analysis is designed for quite a different purpose; it is not necessarily adequate for the purpose of reflecting the cost of raising children in different locations. A very detailed and systematic budgeting of quantities and prices of specific goods and services would be required for that purpose.

Nonetheless, the results presented in Table 3.2 may be interpreted as showing that while the overall farm-nonfarm ratio of 85 percent, as such, probably is acceptable, a latitude of variation is covered by any one ratio. Undoubtedly, in some areas farm families may require as much or more income to achieve the same quantity and quality of goods and services as a nonfarm family in another part of the nation. For example, people residing in isolated rural areas must travel great distances to obtain the specialized medical service of, for example, a gynecologist. High transportation costs also increase the prices of appliances, building materials, food, gasoline, and so forth. The simplifying assumption of a constant ratio probably introduces some distortion into the farm poverty statistics for some locations. This violates Criterion 1 again, although perhaps by a rather minute absolute amount in view of the fact that, according to official census data, fewer than one in ten of the nation's poor reside on farms. Very little if any distortion of the social welfare trends could result from this feature of the poverty definition.

It is important to recognize the leverage of the food-income ratio. For example, if this ratio were shifted from one-third to 30 percent, it would have the immediate effect of raising the poverty line by about 11 percent—a family of four would need $4,378 rather than $3,944 to afford the economy food budget.

J. PATRICK MADDEN

TABLE 3.2 Income Required for Economy Food Plan,
Estimated Ratio of Farm to Other Urbanizations

Urbanization	Assumed value of economy food plan (EFP)[b]	Estimated income required to afford EFP[c]	Ratio farm/other urbanization
Family of 4			
Central city of SMSA	$1018	$3560	85
Noncentral city in urban area of SMSA	1018	3425	88
Urban place[a]	1018	3657	83
Rural nonfarm	1018	3942	77
Rural farm	865	2019	100
Family of 5			
Central city of SMSA	1201	5029	84
Noncentral city in urban area of SMSA	1201	4876	86
Urban place[a]	1201	5137	82
Rural nonfarm	1201	5461	77
Rural farm	1021	4204	100
Family of 6			
Central city of SMSA	1349	4745	79
Noncentral city in urban area of SMSA	1349	4597	82
Urban place[a]	1349	4852	78
Rural nonfarm	1349	5167	73
Rural farm	1146	3761	100

[a]Defined as an urban place having a population of 2,500 to 50,000 outside SMSAs, and similar size places in nonurbanized areas within SMSAs.

[b]One-third of the value of the poverty line. This is a close approximation.

[c]Based on estimated food expenditure function (Carlin 1971) assuming a family of 4, 5, or 6 persons in North Central region; head of household is a white male, age 35 to 64 years, with high school education; age of oldest child 6 to 11 years; age of youngest child less than 6 years; homeowner.

Do families at the poverty level of income spend a third of their income on food? Given the almost infinite variation among poor families, it is clearly absurd to suggest that any one proportion would apply to all. Furthermore, it seems curious and perhaps naive to predicate an income-needs standard entirely on the value of a food budget, completely ignoring the economies and diseconomies tied to family size among the other specific categories of goods and services—transportation, clothing, housing, medical services, etc.—and ignoring the fact that their prices and availability vary sharply from one place and point in time to another.

Let us examine some of the evidence used to establish the proportion of income spent on food by low income families. First it must be recognized that the original one-third ratio was based on the overall national average percent of income spent on food (APF) in 1955. This ratio was then applied to the low income population, under the assumption that each year the poor spend the same proportion of their income on food as the United States population did in 1955. This is clearly a most tenuous assumption. Furthermore, if the ratio is to be conceptually tied to the overall United States ratio, then as the average income level rises and the proportion spent on food declines, the poverty line would be proportionately higher. This presumably was not the intent of those who evolved the poverty definition.

A more direct approach is to ask what proportion of their income the poor typically spend on food. According to food expenditure functions computed from data reported for low income families included in the 1961 Consumer Expenditure Survey (Carlin 1970, USDA 1965), they tend to spend slightly less than a third, or about 30 percent, of their income on food (Table 3.3). Again, considerable variation was observed in this ratio—from 27 to 32 percent in the situations assumed here. A small variation in this ratio is not a trivial issue, given its leverage in determining the poverty thresholds.

Based on the estimated food expenditure function of low income families (Carlin 1971), when real income, including noncash income, is at the poverty line ($3,054 in 1961 for a family of four), food expenditure for a four-person family in a central city is estimated as $950 or 93 percent of the economy food plan value (Table 3.3). Alternatively, an income of $3,560 (or 117 percent of the poverty line) would be required to reach a predicted food expenditure as high as the economy food plan (Table 3.2). Thus, if one assumes the poverty line is

J. PATRICK MADDEN

TABLE 3.3 Ratio of Estimated Food Expenditure to Income

Assumed family characteristics	Income at the poverty line (1961)	Estimated food expenditure[a]	Ratio of food income
Family of 4			
Central city of SMSA	$3054	$950	.31
Noncentral city of SMSA	3054	968	.32
Urban place	3054	937	.31
Rural nonfarm	3054	900	.29
Rural farm	2596	806	.31
Family of 5			
Central city of SMSA	3603	1024	.28
Noncentral city of SMSA	3603	1042	.29
Urban place	3603	1011	.28
Rural nonfarm	3603	974	.27
Rural farm	3063	836	.27
Family of 6			
Central city of SMSA	4046	1263	.31
Noncentral city of SMSA	4046	1280	.32
Urban place	4046	1250	.31
Rural nonfarm	4046	1213	.30
Rural farm	3439	1104	.32

[a]Estimated from food expenditure function reported by Carlin (1971). See table 2 for detailed assumptions.

the income needed to afford the economy food plan, given the expenditure patterns exhibited by low income families, an income higher than the present poverty line would be required.

Even if a somewhat higher ratio were adopted as the overall national ratio, however, a multitude of individual variations are covered. For example, elderly families with no children may tend to spend a lower proportion of their income on food, as compared to a family with teenage children. Families with extraordinary medical expenses or other needs would require far more income than three times the value of the economy food plan. Conversely, a rather self-sufficient family with relatively low expenses would need less. These variations are naturally obscured in any tabulations of aggregate data. Furthermore, any cnanges in the ratio over time are completely assumed away when a fixed ratio is used.

Even if the second, third, and fourth premises of the poverty line definition are accepted, however, the validity of the first premise is still open to question: how "adequate" is the level of living represented by the poverty line? This question is of singular importance to the conceptual validity of the poverty data as indicators of social welfare. This discussion of the other premises is mere nit-picking by comparison.

How does one judge the adequacy of a poverty standard? How can social accountants decide whether the poverty line reflects the lower limit of adequacy, below which an acute problem of social welfare prevails? Some reasonable basis for comparison must be agreed upon before poverty data can be interpreted as indicators of social welfare, either at one point in time (Criterion 1), or as a trend (Criterion 2).

First, the poverty line should be viewed within the broad historical perspective. Second, it is necessary to recognize the distinction between relative and absolute deprivation. And, finally, the poverty line should be compared with some objective measure of income needs.

In tracing the history of public welfare in England and America since the eighteenth century, Coll (1969) cites a somewhat erratic, gradual liberalization over the centuries, despite significant "roll-backs" from time to time. For example, Coll states that medieval poor law, as administered mainly by the Catholic Church, was predicated on the idea that poverty was not a crime, that a poor man was an honorable man, and that the destitute had a right to assistance as a matter of justice. It was made clear, though, that the "able-bodied idler" should be urged to work rather than encouraged by handouts. However, the

J. PATRICK MADDEN

prevailing ideas about poverty changed drastically and in 1388 the first Settlement Law was enacted, whereby able-bodied beggars were punished. All migrants were deemed criminals.

Despite the widespread acceptance of the Calvinist concept of poverty—that poverty resulted from a failure of character—in the late eighteenth century, there were some isolated attempts to make the treatment of the poor more humane. In 1796, for example, a wage supplement law was enacted in Speenhamland, England. The income support was based on the size of the family and was adjusted according to the current price of bread. This was the ancient predecessor of today's official poverty definition, which provides price level adjustments based on a wide range of consumer goods and services.

At this point in Anglo-American history, the typical level of support was set below the lowest going wage, with the implied purpose of preventing idleness. This same miserable level of aid was applied generally to all cases—the aged, the helplessly sick, orphans, and the unemployed. The main criterion for establishing a needs standard seemed to be the minimization of public costs. In New York in 1800, for example, indigent persons were passed from one part of the state to another to prevent any increase in local poor taxes.

As the general level of affluence increased, so did the concept of minimum needs. In 1906, Ryan proposed the "living wage" as a minimum standard for all American families (Coll 1969). Ryan's standard, set at $600 for an "average family" or as much as $650-$800 in a high cost urban area, would cover the cost of "decent food, clothing and shelter," plus medical care, insurance, education, recreation, and savings. This concept is embodied in the modern Bureau of Labor Statistics (BLS) budgets for a family of four, as discussed later.

Recent evidence supports the conclusion that the official Census Bureau poverty line is below currently held concepts of adequacy. In a survey in an "average income county" (near Indianapolis) two samples of the population were interviewed—reputed "leaders" in the county, and a general representative sample (Potter et al. 1969). In part of the interview, respondents were asked "How would you define poverty?" The most frequent responses had to do with economic and environmental conditions, "When people don't have enough coal to be comfortable . . . don't eat . . . wear rags . . . don't know where the next meal is coming from . . . people who don't have enough money to pay rent and bills or not a job, at least a good job. . . . " The next most frequent type of response had to do with social conditions. As expected, some of the respondents reflected the usual stereotypes of poverty. "Poverty is mostly lazy people unwilling to work, rough living conditions...." Some cited inability to work and various patterns of poverty throughout a person's lifetime. When asked what they felt the minimum income levels were for a family of four, the community leader sample indicated a much lower level ($4,040 median response) than did the general survey sample ($5,002) (Potter 1969:9). It is worth noting, however, that even the more conservative estimate is considerably above the poverty line.

Prevailing concepts of income adequacy and relative deprivation also change over time. Some societies, particularly Western societies, have been characterized as being on a "hedonistic treadmill." That is, as individuals find themselves better off in period two than they were in period one, their aspiration for further improvement in period three tends to make them dissatisfied with the improvement already experienced. This syndrome has serious implications with regard to interpretation of income distribution data.

For example, Easterlin (1973) found a positive relation between "happiness" and income in each of thirty national population surveys he examined. Eleven of these surveys were done in the United States; the other nineteen were done in other countries, including three communist nations and eleven countries in Asia, Africa, and Latin America. This relationship held up only within countries, and not between countries. When you compare rich and poor countries, or higher and lower income situations in a given country at two different times, the happiness differences one might expect on the basis of differences in income do not appear.

Easterlin offers an explanation for this paradox. He suggests the answer lies in the way people form their value judgments regarding their criteria for happiness. "The satisfaction one gets from his material situation depends not on the absolute amount of goods he has, but on how this amount compares with what he thinks he needs." He points out that the great majority of Americans have a level of living that would have been considered wealthy two centuries ago. Nonetheless, the typical American today does not consider himself wealthy by contemporary standards. Economic growth and rising incomes are accompanied by an upward shift in perceived needs, which tends to offset the positive effect an increase in income would have otherwise.

Poverty, in any of its various dimensions, can be defined either in relative or in absolute terms. People have basic physical needs for food, clothing, shelter, and medical care, and when these are not met, a person is "in need," in an absolute sense. Whether or not these basic needs are met, however, a person may or may not feel "relatively deprived," for this is a function of one's position vis-à-vis his reference group in that particular cultural setting and point in history. Veterans of the Depression, for example, have been heard to say, "We were hungry but we didn't feel poor, because none of the neighbors had enough to eat either." In contrast, today's poor see about them (on television, in magazines, etc.) conspicuous overconsumption, and they feel their deprivation more acutely.

The paradox of relative versus absolute deprivation is frequently seen throughout the country. Consider for a moment two families about equally deprived in money terms—family A has an income 25 percent below the poverty line, while family B's income is 10 percent below the poverty line. Family A lives in an area of widespread poverty, while family B lives in an area with few poor families. Both families may be absolutely deprived in terms of access to services; family A because services are nonexistent, and family B because it cannot afford to pay for the services. However, family B has slightly more income and it may benefit from free services provided by the rich community; thus, it may be better off in an absolute sense. But in relative terms the opposite would be true: the poor family in a rich area is likely to feel much more deprived than the family with the same income surrounded by other poor families.

The same kind of distinction exists between relative and absolute deprivation with regard to housing, health care, and other services. Poor people in isolated rural areas surrounded by other poor people may be lacking in all the "necessities" of life, but not feel as deprived (in a relative sense) as they feel when they move in among more affluent neighbors whose children are better fed and clothed, and whose medical, dental, and other needs have been attended to regularly by highly paid specialists. Let us focus on income as one of the key dimensions of poverty. The current official poverty definition embodies an absolute standard—absolute in the sense that it represents a constant level of purchasing power from one year to the next, independent of trends in the affluence of society as a whole. At present there is no plan to modify this level. Thus, the historical trend toward progressively higher standards of adequacy may be, at least for the foreseeable future, ignored by the "official" standards and the poverty data forthcoming from the federal government. Presumably the national standard of living will continue its upward trend, despite temporary delays due to recession. A necessary result of using an absolute standard is that it will represent a relatively lower standard over time, as long as economic growth and prosperity prevail.

In an attempt to keep the poverty lines commensurate with the overall level of prosperity, relative standards of poverty have been advocated. One example is an income level at one-half of the national median family income (Table 3.4). This measure is quite simple, with no adjustments for family size or farm residence. Using this measure, the percentage of families in the United States counted as "poor" has changed very little in the past decade—dropping from about 20 to 18 percent. Meanwhile the percentage of the population in poverty according to the absolute standard of the official Census Bureau definition has dropped by roughly half, from about 20 to 10 percent. Thus, we see a marked discrepancy between the two series. The official trends seem, at face value, to be encouraging; year after year fewer families are unable to afford the fixed level of consumption implied by the poverty thresholds. The relative trends, being almost static, indicate no significant change in the percentage of the population participating in the rising national level of affluence. Thus, in a relative sense, the poverty situation has shown little, if any, improvement.

Proponents of the relative standards of poverty recognize that frustration is a function of the gap between aspirations and expectations. Aspirations of the less well-to-do tend to rise as they observe the ever-increasing affluence of their reference groups. For example, judging by the apparently increasing discontent among the urban poor, it appears that their aspirations are rising even faster than the expectation of increases in welfare payments and other income. This may be partly the result of the need-stimulating advertisements of television, magazines, and the like. As the poor are led to wish for more and more "gadgets of progress," aspirations far outstrip expectations of gain, based on their income situations and on their prospects for social mobility.

Herein lies a potential source of dissension: while society as a whole may be lulled into complacency by the official poverty data reflecting a steadily improving situation (based on an absolute standard of poverty),

J. PATRICK MADDEN

TABLE 3.4 Poverty Trends 1959 to 1970

		Poverty line		Percent poor based on standards	
Year	Adjustment for C.P.I. (1969=100)	Absolute (Census Bureau[a])	Relative (M/2)[b]	Absolute (Census Bureau[c])	Relative (M/2)
1970	106.0	$3968	$4941	11.0(14.2)%	18.8%
1969	100.0	3743	4724	10.5(14.2)	18.4
1968	94.9	3552	4321	11.3	18.1
1967	91.9	3410	3991	12.5	18.5
1966	88.6	3316	3723	13.1(14.2)	19.3
1965	86.1	3223	3482	(15.8)	19.9
1964	84.7	3170	3288	(17.4)	20.1
1963	83.6	3129	3130	(17.9)	19.7
1962	82.5	3088	2985	(19.4)	19.7
1961	81.6	3054	2873	(20.3)	20.4
1960	80.7	3021	2815	(20.7)	20.0
1959	79.5	2976	2714	(20.8)	19.7

Sources: Census Bureau poverty figures are from P-60 No. 76. The relative poverty data were calculated from primary family data published in: P-60, No. 75, page 28; and P-60, No. 80, page 57. The data reported here are an updated and revised version of similar data reported elsewhere (Fuchs 1969, President's Commission on Income Maintenance 1969).

[a]Shown in this column as an example is the official poverty threshold in constant 1969 dollars for a nonfarm family of 4, adjusted from 1969 by Consumer Price Index, as shown in first column.

[b]One-half the national median income of primary families (excluding individuals living alone or with unrelated persons). The average size of "poor" families is about 4 persons, according to the Census Bureau definition of poverty.

[c]Percent of families reporting current annual income less than the official poverty line. Numbers in parentheses are based on unrevised Census Bureau procedures.

the poor may perceive their situation as worsening. Those of us who are asked to produce or interpret poverty data should bear in mind that at any point in history, society's concept of what constitutes a minimum acceptable level of living seems to be a function of the general level of prosperity. As a nation becomes richer, the definition of subsistence seems to rise.

Despite these considerations, however, absolute standards of deprivation also have an important role to play in indicating the current status and trends in social welfare. The nutritional and biochemical standards used in the National Nutrition Survey (U.S. Senate 1970) to detect evidence of malnutrition are essentially absolute standards. Census statistics on prevalence of dilapidated and substandard housing are another example. Trends in the incidence of inadequacy vis-à-vis these absolute standards are unquestionably meaningful, as far as they go. The official poverty statistics, indicating the number of families unable to afford an absolute level of consumption of goods and services, are equally valuable when interpreted properly. These absolute standards can and should be compared with some objective measure of income needs, for example, the BLS budgets.

The BLS calculates the cost of meeting the needs of a family of four persons, based on three alternative life styles (U.S. Bureau of Labor Statistics 1969). The lowest of the three budget levels, called the "Lower Standard," is designed to "meet the requirements for physical health and social well-being of family members, the nurture of children, and participation in community activities." The two higher budgets (the Moderate and Higher) are based on somewhat more liberal consumption levels.

In Table 3.5 the BLS Lower Standard is compared with a budget proposed for a family of four at the poverty line. The poverty budget, overall, falls one-third short of the BLS Lower Standard. This particular poverty budget contains enough money to supply virtually the full need for clothing and personal care, but it meets only 89 percent of the food needs and 83 percent of the housing needs assumed by BLS to provide a minimum decent life style. There is little allowance in the poverty budget for transportation or recreation, and nothing at all for medical or life insurance expenses.

Thus, assuming the BLS Lower Standard is a reflection of the money needed to buy the necessities of modern American life (alternative assumptions, either higher or lower, could be made), the official pov-

J. PATRICK MADDEN

TABLE 3.5. Monthly Budgets for the Poor, 1967

Consumption item	Poverty line[a]	BLS lower standard	Poverty as percent of BLS lower standard
Food	$122	$137	89%
Housing	91	109	83
Transportation	6	37	16
Clothing and personal care	57	58	98
Medical care	- -	39	0
Gifts and contributions	- -	12	0
Personal life insurance	- -	10	0
Other family consumption[b]	9	25	36
Total, per month	284	427	67
Total, per year	3410	5127	67

Sources: U.S. Bureau Labor Statistics, 1969:6; President's Commission on Income Maintenance, 1969:14.

[a]The breakdown by consumption categories (food, clothing, etc.) is based on budgeted need for an AFDC family of 4 in Los Angeles, California.

[b]Recreation, education, tobacco, etc.

erty line is found to be grossly inadequate. This fact must be kept in mind in interpreting the official poverty data, indicating the number of "poor." The number with inadequate income, based on the BLS standard, is considerably higher.

DEPRIVATION AS A CONTINUUM

The poverty thresholds are frequently used as an income "needs standard" in administering antipoverty programs. Certainly those persons below the poverty line are worse off than those just above it, other things being equal. But the way the poverty line is used as an eligibility criterion seems to imply that those a dollar above the poverty level are by some magic placed beyond the range of deprivation. As noted by

Wilber in chapter 1, deprivation is a continuous, rather than a discrete, variable.

In the preceding discussion focusing on inadequate income (one dimension of poverty) it is clear that the official poverty definition represents a wholly inadequate level of living. It is inadequate today, according to current absolute standards, and it is guaranteed by its very nature to become less adequate with the passage of time, as the national level of affluence rises. The poverty line does not infallibly distinguish between the happily contented citizens and the miserable paupers. The risk of experiencing serious inadequacies is much greater among people at the low end of the income continuum, but this risk does not end abruptly at the poverty line. The same is true of other dimensions of poverty; and families somewhat above the poverty line are also deprived, even in absolute terms, with respect to the other dimensions of poverty as well.

In the following discussion two major points are emphasized: (1) that deprivation, according to several different dimensions, is most severe among families with very low income, and (2) that this deprivation does not terminate at the poverty line, or at any level established by similar measures of income inadequacy. For this purpose, close examination will be made of three reflections of the health of the poor: incidence of malnutrition, frequency and length of periods of illness, and death rates.

An obvious linkage exists between the level of a family's food intake and its health; equally obvious is the linkage between ill health and ability to perform jobs required to earn an income.

Inadequate nutrition is found in all strata of society, but it is most widespread among the poor. No reliable statistics are yet available on the extent of hunger and undernutrition among the poor, but this is clearly one of the significant sources of the health problems among the poor. Outright starvation due to marasmus and kwashiorkor is rare in the United States, yet there is damage in more subtle forms. For example, the National Nutrition Survey has found widespread incidence of physical underdevelopment and malformation resulting from nutritional inadequacies (U.S. Senate 1970). Evidence of brain damage has also been detected. Other studies have demonstrated clearly the detrimental effect of malnutrition on the brain development and subsequent mental ability of children (Birren and Hess 1968). Thus, a vicious cycle occurs: the poor cannot afford adequate food and other health services;

J. PATRICK MADDEN

this causes subsequent health problems such as physical and mental difficulties that inhibit the ability to earn and thus cause low income, and the cycle is repeated. Different people may enter the cycle at different stages. For example, a family may become "poor" due to the death or illness of the breadwinner—or even his prolonged unemployment, as in the case of many thousands of Appalachian coal miners. Once caught in the cycle, unending generations of a family may remain destitute. Alternatively, families may be able to break out of the poverty cycle when adequate opportunities and social services are available to help overcome the critical impediments to progress.

Over a long period, an inadequate diet can lead to poor nutrition and deteriorating health. Almost by definition, the poor lack enough resources to afford an adequate diet, since the poverty line is based on the value of the economy food plan. The authors of the economy food plan clearly reject the proposition that it represents an adequate diet for the typical poor family. Rather, it is designed to provide an adequate diet under very special conditions and assumes that: (1) it is for a very short-term emergency situation (U.S. Bureau of the Census 1969), and (2) the homemaker has the required shopping and cooking skills needed to obtain the proper foods and prepare them in a way that will be both economical and palatable to the family. Neither of these conditions is consistent with the facts. Families whose food expenditure is at the economy food plan level fail in nine out of ten cases to have a "good" diet—one supplying National Research Council (NRC) allowances of seven key nutrients.

Based on a nationwide survey in 1968, Lansing and Dickinson (1970:11) showed that one in five children in the United States is a member of a family which eats less than the economy food plan recommends. Nearly half of the black children are found in families with such low levels of food consumption.

Tabulations of data from another national survey show clearly the principle that dietary deprivation is a continuum which is most severe at very low income levels, and declines gradually in intensity as income rises above the poverty level (Figure 3.2). The percentage of incidence of inadequate food expenditure is highest among the poorest of the poor—80 percent of families with incomes less than three-fourths of the poverty line figure spent less on food than the value of the economy food plan (EFP). About two in every three families (63 percent) just below the poverty line had food expenditure below the EFP, compared

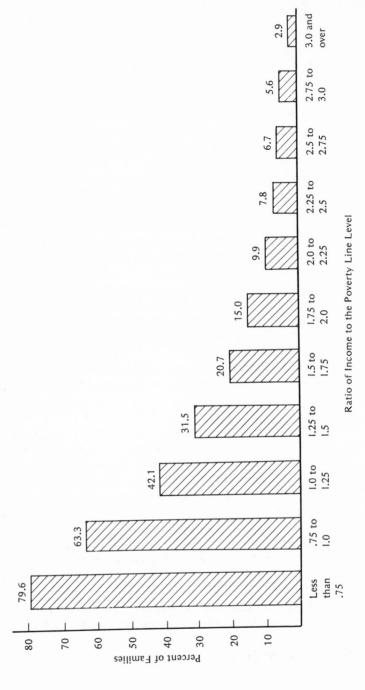

FIGURE 3.2   Families with Food Expenditure below the Value of the Economy Food Plan, U.S., 1961

with 42 percent of those just above the poverty line. Not until incomes reach twice the poverty line figure does the incidence of such low food expenditure drop below 10 percent.

These data do not represent the incidence of hunger and malnutrition, but only a low cash value of food consumed. Poor diets over time usually lead to poor nutrition, but they are not synonymous. There is no direct and accurate way to use these data to reflect the extent of hunger and malnutrition—physical and biochemical tests are needed also (Clark 1969, U.S. Senate 1970). Furthermore, because of variations in human behavior, not all families spending a given level of money on food will have equally adequate diets or nutritional status. Nonetheless, the tabulations clearly indicate the principle that deprivation is a continuum extending beyond the poverty line.

Other tabulations of this same data show that while food expenditures are slightly more equally distributed than income, the poor have a disproportionately small share of the nation's food. For example, let us compare families at the opposite ends of the income continuum—those below the poverty line versus those whose incomes exceed three times the figure at the poverty line: The poorest 14 percent of all families get 4 percent of the income and 7 percent of the food. The richest 23 percent of all families get 41 percent of the income and 32 percent of the food.

These findings show clearly that the poorest of the poor are severely deprived of food, in the relative as well as the absolute sense. It is also clear that the degree of deprivation declines only gradually as income rises above the poverty line.

The axiom that wealth can't buy good health and long life seems to apply only to the upper income classes. Among the people at the lower end of the income scale there is a very definite relationship between poverty and health (Kosa et al. 1969, Lerner 1969). For example, studies on morbidity conducted by the National Institutes of Health show clearly that the poor are more often sick, and that they tend to lose a greater number of days from work due to illness (Table 3.6). When illness is measured in terms of bed-disability days or restricted activity days, the lowest income category (under $3,000) is found to be affected more than twice as much as the highest category ($7,000 and over). The middle income category ($3,000 to $6,999) also has substantially worse health (18 to 54 percent higher) than the upper group. A more gradual continuum is apparent when illness is measured in terms

TABLE 3.6   Health Characteristics by Income Class & Color, U.S. (July 1965-June 1967)

| Health indicator | Days per person per year, by family income: | | |
	Low (under $3,000)	Medium ($3,000 to $6,999)	High ($7,000 and over)
	Days		
Days disabled and in bed:[a]			
White	10.2	5.8	4.9
Nonwhite	9.3	5.4	3.5
Days lost from work:[b]			
White	7.4	6.3	4.7
Nonwhite	8.0	7.0	4.8
Restricted activity days:[c]			
White	28.9	15.1	12.5
Nonwhite	21.0	12.1	9.3
	Percent of High Income Group		
Days disabled and in bed:[a]			
White	208	118	100
Nonwhite	266	154	100
Days lost from work:[b]			
White	157	134	100
Nonwhite	167	146	100
Restricted activity days:[c]			
White	231	121	100
Nonwhite	226	130	100

Source: U.S. Department of Health, Education, and Welfare 1969.
[a]Number of bed disability days per person per year.
[b]Per currently employed person per year.
[c]Ambulatory sick or injured; able to work only at substantially reduced level due to specific illness or injury.

J. PATRICK MADDEN

of number of days lost from work (per currently employed person per year). The middle income category has about 40 percent more days lost from work, compared with about 60 percent more among the lowest income category. (Nonwhites appear to have generally worse health than whites in each income interval.)

A question of causality is apparent in the morbidity data. Are the families poor because they are sick and out of work, or sick because of years of deprivation, inadequate diets, and lack of medical service? Undoubtedly both forces are acting simultaneously. Before the effects of poverty per se on the health of the poor family can be determined, data reflecting the long term histories of the health and income of families are required.

The relation between poverty and death rates for the population as a whole is very hard to determine directly, owing to lack of appropriate data. Death rates are tabulated for infants (under 1 year of age) by family income, but indirect evidence must be used for older age classes.

The infant mortality rate is considerably higher among families with lower incomes (Table 3.7). Compared with families with over $5,000 income, the infant mortality rate is nearly 50 percent higher among the lowest income class, with the intermediate income class ($3,000 to $4,999) halfway in between. This is an example of the continuum of deprivation—that the problems rampant among the poor are also visited upon the near-poor, although with somewhat lower frequency.

Why are the infant mortality rates so much higher among the poor? Several possible explanations may be offered. The first, and perhaps most obvious, is that the poor simply lack sufficient income to buy the goods and services needed to prevent sickness. Severe inadequacies have been found in the availability of food (as discussed earlier), clothing, shelter, and preventive medical care. The poor have fewer preventive medical and dental services, relying mainly on therapeutic treatment (Doherty 1970, National Advisory Commission on Rural Poverty 1967). Prenatal child care is often omitted; the low income mother often sees the doctor only once—at the time of delivery. This results in more frequent complications for the mother and child. The poor seldom see the dentist for preventive care and fillings, more frequently for extractions. These facts may be attributed partly to the inadequacy of income, and partly also to location, since many of the poor live in poor communities and isolated rural areas, where health and other social services are usually inadequate. This is the natural result of the

TABLE 3.7   Infant Mortality Rate by Family Income, U.S.

Family income	Infant mortality rate per 1,000 live births
Under $3,000	31.8
$ 3,000 to $4,999	24.9
5,000 to 6,999	17.9
7,000 to 9,999	19.6
10,000 and over	19.6

Source: U.S. Department of Health, Education and Welfare 1970:5.

operation of Keynes's Law—that demand creates its own supply. By definition, the poor lack the purchasing power to translate their needs into effective demand. The market for medical services (as for other goods and services) remains inadequate in poor areas because there is not enough purchasing power there to bid against the more affluent locations for the limited supply of medical personnel. This is a pernicious aspect of relative deprivation. The richer the rest of society gets, the more effectively it can outbid the less fortunate segments of society.

Infant mortality rates vary greatly among the states, owing to variations in the incidence of poverty, the availability and use of health services, and other factors. Calculations by the Public Health Service indicate that "if the infant mortality rate of each state had been as low as that of the best state (in 1967) 20,579 babies would not have died during their first year." (U.S. Department of Health, Education, and Welfare 1970:6). How many of these deaths are attributable to poverty? How many babies would not have died in the United States last year if the infant mortality rates for the poor and near-poor were as low as for the higher income classes? What about persons in other age classes? This grim "body count" of poverty is impossible to determine accurately with currently available data.

An indirect indication of a portion of this body count can be deduced from unpublished data from the Census Bureau's Current Population Surveys. Consider the trends in the number of children in the cohort of "age less than 16" in 1968 (1 to 16 in 1969). Sixteen

TABLE 3.8 Disappearance of Children in a Specific Age, Cohort, by Education of Head of Household, U.S., 1968 to 1969

Age and year	All	In families whose head has less than 9 years education
	Thousands	*Thousands*
Under age 16 in 1968	63,158	14,059
1 to 16 years in 1969	63,108	13,587
Change, number	50	472
Change, percent	0.08%	3.36%

Source: Unpublished tables from Census Bureau, "Tables for OEO from CPS March Supplement" based on March 1969 and March 1970 Current Population Surveys. Tabulations dated August 1970 and November 1970.

percent of these children were in poor families in 1968. Between 1968 and 1969, their overall numbers declined very little (less than a tenth of one percent), presumably due to the low death rate of persons of this age (Table 3.8).

However, those in families headed by a person with less than nine years education were different in two respects: 36 percent were in poor families, and there was a 3.4 percent decline in their numbers from 1968 to 1969. The total "disappearance" was more than 470,000 persons. If the average rate of decline were to prevail in this class, the reduction would have been only about 11,000. Of course, this is only an approximation. A more refined analysis based on income-specific death rates would be required to get a satisfactory estimate. Nonetheless, these results give a rough idea of the vast magnitude of the problem.

How can the "disappearance" of so many children from families headed by a person with low education level be explained? Is it merely a statistical quirk? Sample error may account for part of the difference. The Current Population Surveys are designed to achieve other objectives, and may not be adequate for this purpose. These findings should be checked against other sources of data for other years, preferably with large samples designed for the purpose. It is also theoretically possible that during the year some of these children were reclassified due to the family head completing his ninth year of schooling; others would have "left home." However, it seems very unlikely that any of these factors would explain *all* of the disappearance. It seems reasonable to conclude that part of the disappearance may be due to the cumulative effects of a higher incidence of poverty—inadequate housing and food, lack of medical services, and other hardships—which make children more likely to die at an early age.

Herein lies one of the major challenges to our society—to provide the means of maintaining adequate health—including food, shelter, and medical services to all persons—regardless of income.

TOWARD AN ALTERNATIVE POVERTY MEASURE

Even if the poverty level of income should be raised to a more generous amount such as the BLS Lower Standard, problems of accuracy and relevance would remain. A comprehensive analysis of the problems and possibilities for improvement is beyond the scope of the present paper. For purposes of illustration only one problem is discussed here, and a possible solution is suggested.

Each year thousands of families who are counted as "poor" (because of their low current income) have rather affluent life styles, as indicated by their high level of consumption and assets. Some of these are recent college graduates whose jobs begin late in the year. Others are wealthy businessmen who experience a temporary and unexpected net loss during the year. People such as these have unusual or permanent incomes far above the poverty line (Friedman 1957). If the poverty criterion were permanent income rather than annual or current income, cases such as these would not be counted in the poverty statistics. Likewise, families having a windfall gain just enough to push them temporarily over the poverty line for one year would still be counted as poor on the basis of their permanent income.

Poverty data based on permanent income rather than current income would more accurately gauge the extent of impoverished life styles, though other conceptual problems would remain unsolved. Some of the problems deserving attention are: how to treat the family's assets and changes in inventory; "secondary" poverty, characterized by inability

J. PATRICK MADDEN

of middle income families to afford necessities, due to overspending on luxuries or other consumption; how to account for receipt of noncash items that substitute for money income; or how to make allowances for extraordinary medical expenses or other costs that drastically reduce a family's life style.

Clearly, much more research is needed to develop a fully acceptable measure, even for the income dimension of poverty.

4 Migration and Poverty

Thomas R. Panko

For centuries, migration has been a major means by which people seek solutions to their problems; the mass movement of peoples from economically depressed areas to areas that hold greater promise is legendary. Politically or religiously oppressed peoples—refugees and displaced persons—have fled to escape their oppressors.

In the United States, the well-known movements to the West and to the cities have predominated historically and are still much in evidence today. Millions of Americans, for example, have moved from the old plantation South and from Appalachia in search of better opportunities. The mass movement from the South to northern industrial centers began in the 1920s as a result of the demand for industrial workers. The shortage of laborers in northern industry was largely the result of quota restrictions imposed on immigrants from abroad. Migrants from the South, both white and black, were essentially substituted for the European immigrants. The South-to-North movement regained momentum during and after World War II. By the 1960s, however, there were also signs of substantial movements into the South. For recent years there are clear signs of movements to coastal locations as well as to metropolitan centers. A major part of present migration within the United States is movement between urban areas.

Even in areas that are not especially depressed, low income and unemployed persons and families often move in an effort to improve their circumstances. Migrant farm workers represent a different variety of migrant, although they too try to solve their problems by moving. They move more or less continuously with the changing seasons and the harvesting of crops; it is largely a matter of moving with their work as a means of survival. Hence, while migration per se is not restricted to persons in poverty or to problems of poverty areas, migration and poverty have some obvious connections.

Relationships between poverty and migration are the focus of attention in this and the following chapter. The present chapter begins with a brief look at the principle of migration selectivity. Then the framework of relationships among resources, mobilization, and poverty properties, presented in chapter 2, is extended and applied more specifically to migration, for both individuals and communities. Appalachian migration is examined as an example to show the scope of the migration issue, focusing on implications both for sending and for receiving areas. Based on what is known about relationships between migration and poverty, and on what needs to be known, concluding observations concentrate on some prospects for research. The discussion of poverty and migration continues in chapter 5, which focuses on programs intended to reduce problems of migrants.

SELECTION OF MIGRANTS

Migration is closely related to the life cycle of individuals, and to their status. It is clear that one cannot control age, sex, and color, yet educational attainment, employment, occupation, income, and marital status are subject to personal initiative and action as well as to social policies and programs. The possession of certain characteristics whether inherited or acquired has a bearing on one's chances for migration.

Individuals tend to be selected for migration on the basis of age, sex, color, education, income, employment status, occupation, marital status, and other characteristics. The principle of migration selectivity has been thoroughly established by demographers and social scientists. Since Ravenstein (1885, 1889) published his laws of migration, the overwhelming evidence has indicated that persons with particular traits are more likely to be singled out for migration.

It is evident that young adults are more migratory than persons at other age levels. Specifically, migration rates for the United States indicate that mobility is greatest in young adulthood (18-34, with a median age of about 22). In an achievement-oriented society this is an especially critical point in the life cycle of young people for it is the time when they are in the process of establishing themselves—getting married, starting their careers, and seeking the best living opportunities.

In contrast to the popular notion that migrants are generally unmarried persons leaving farms or small towns to seek their fortunes in the big city, data from the 1970 census show that a higher proportion of married persons than single were migrants. With only this data it is difficult to explain why married persons should be more highly selected for migration. It may be that migrants more frequently move as family units or tend to marry at earlier ages.

Bogue and Hagood's (1953) study of differential migration in the corn and cotton belts represents a major pioneering investigation of the socioeconomic selectivity of internal migration. Using the newly instituted item on migration in the 1940 census, they were able to arrive at several findings relating to socioeconomic status (here measured in terms of educational attainment, occupation, and income). The magnitude of their study permits only the presentation of those findings deemed most relevant to this paper.

Migration to cities was found to be highly and positively selective with respect to educational attainment. "In addition to selecting those persons who were better educated than persons of the same age at the place of origin, it also selected persons who were better educated than persons of the same age at the place of destination" (Bogue and Hagood 1953:57). Two exceptions were a group of migrants from farm areas and nonwhite migrants from the cotton belt.

Migration was also strongly selective of occupation. Among migrants to cities from other urban areas, a disproportionately small number were concentrated in unskilled or semiskilled occupations in comparison both to sending and to receiving populations (Bogue and Hagood 1953:91); migrants between cities tended to be selected for white-collar occupations. As was true for educational attainment, migrants from farms were concentrated in the lower status levels (referring to unskilled occupations).

A third general finding of the study pertains to migration selectivity on the basis of income. As Bogue and Hagood (1953:91-101) point out, "In theory, one of the strong incentives to migrate is the desire to increase money income. Hence, it would be possible to reason that the segment of the population most likely to migrate would be the part that receives small income." The findings do not fully support this theory. Actually, persons in the middle income groups were selected most positively and intensely. Further, in comparison to the receiving population, a larger proportion of young migrants to cities from urban areas was in the lower and middle income range, with a small number at either end of the income scale.

These findings suggest migrants are typically of higher socioeconomic status than nonmigrants in both receiving and sending populations. This contrasts with a study conducted in North Carolina by C. Horace Hamilton (1958:116-22). Hamilton utilized two different methodological approaches to study the educational selectivity of rural-urban migration for the period 1940-50. The residual-survival rate method was used in the first approach. The survival rate method of determining the amount of migration in a given area involves estimating the number of people at one census point expected to be alive and residing in the same location at the following census. This method assumes no migration occurred. The predicted number of survivors is subtracted from the actual population count at the second census point, the difference being an estimate of the net number of migrants. This procedure is applied to each age group. The major finding was that migration from the state and from rural farm areas was most selective of persons in extreme educational levels and least selective of those in middle educational levels.

The second approach, however, based on sample surveys of two entirely rural counties, did not indicate a tendency to select so heavily from the extreme educational levels. The most relevant finding was that rates of migration from rural areas increase with education. Although this is another example of a study conducted within relatively confined geographic boundaries, the findings are generally supportive of the Bogue-Hagood study.

Shryock and Nam (1965:301-02) used data from the 1940 and 1950 censuses to relate educational attainment and migration. Their major finding was that migrants leaving a region exhibited a higher median level of educational attainment than persons who did not move out of the region. This relationship held without exception for all age-sex groups.

Another study relating education to migration was conducted by Suval and Hamilton (1965:546). Using 1960 census data, they found, "Migrant populations include proportionally more of the better educated persons than nonmigrant populations regardless of sex, age, color, or direction of movement to and from the South and its divisions." More specifically, the educational selectivity of net migration from the South is greatest among young adults, Negroes, and males.

Although the studies cited thus far employed different indicators of socioeconomic status for comparing migrants and nonmigrants, they display a definite consistency: migrants tend to be of higher status (in terms of educational attainment, occupation, and income) than nonmigrants.

These studies have done much to document the characteristics of those who do migrate. Of even greater importance to this study, however, is the exploration of the factors influencing the decision to migrate, and the connection between migration and poverty. The framework of relationships among resources, mobilization, and poverty properties presented in chapter 2 can be extended and applied to the issue of migration, both for individuals and for communities.

POVERTY PROPERTIES AND MIGRATION

An extension of the resource-mobilization-property model to individuals as movers or nonmovers is shown in Table 4.1. It must be noted that the distinction between mover and stayer is tenuous in the sense that over a period of time large proportions of a population change their place of residence. Over the life cycle, Americans tend to migrate across county lines a total of about four times on the average (Wilber 1963). Therefore a person classed as a stayer during one year may be a mover the next, and vice versa. In Table 4.1, health is shown as a basic resource of individuals, the use of health services and facilities is viewed as the mobilization of resources, and physical and mental handicaps illustrate poverty properties in relationship to migration. In the case of a mover, a handicap may impede or prevent a reasonable or satisfactory adjustment of the individual at his destination. The extent to which the handicap becomes an impediment to adjustment depends on the nature and severity of the handicap and on how well the individual can control or reduce the effects of the handicap on his adjustment. Through his own efforts and through accessibility, availability, and utilization of services and facilities, migrants with handicaps achieve some degree of control over their adjustments. In some instances, a primary motivation to move to a new community is to seek better health services or vocational rehabilitation programs.

THOMAS R. PANKO

TABLE 4.1 Poverty Properties of Movers and Nonmovers

Basic resources	Mobilization	Poverty properties	
		Mover	Stayer
Health	Use of services and facilities	Handicap hindering or preventing adjustment	Handicap discouraging or preventing adjustment or move
Capability	Education and training	Lack of appropriate skills at destination	Underdeveloped skills hindering adjustment or move
Motivation	Goal achievement	Obstacles to achievement of goals at destination	Obstacles to goal attainment, including relocation
Personality	Socialization	Inappropriate or inadequate socialization for destination	Inappropriate or inadequate socialization
Socioeconomic status	Achievement of status	Obstacles to achievement of higher status at destination	Unsuccessful status-achievement and inability to move
Kinship bonds	Extended family integration and interaction	Interference with or severance of kinship ties as a result of migrating	Malfunctioning or broken family ties

As stayers, handicapped individuals often suffer from low income, unemployment, and other properties of poverty in conjunction with their handicap. In contrast with the handicapped mover, the stayer may be discouraged or effectively prevented from moving to a new community largely because of his handicap. If the mobilization of health services and facilities is inadequate in the stayer's home community, he may never escape from his particular kind of poverty. In this event the handicapped stayer is likely to be permanently trapped and can only hope that improved services and facilities are forthcoming.

In the course of separation from one community and resettlement in another, the mental health of migrants is influenced by the amount and kind of stress involved in moving. In the historical settlement of the western frontier, it was often said that cowards never started and weaklings never arrived. This line of thought would suggest that communities built up heavily from migration would manifest great mental and physical vigor. Odegaard (1932) demonstrated just the opposite effect when he found that Norwegian emigrants overseas had higher rates of hospitalization for mental disorders than Norwegians remaining in Norway. Malzberg and Lee (1956) found a similar situation in the state of New York, where the rate of first admissions to mental hospitals was higher for migrants from other states than for native New Yorkers.

Precisely why migrants appear to be more prone to mental illness is not certain although, as Bogue (1969) points out, there are several plausible hypotheses: (1) nonmigrants suffer less stress than migrants and therefore have lower rates of mental disorder; (2) individuals in a state of mental strain and those who are seriously maladjusted tend to seek an escape; (3) migrants without families may be more easily detected and hospitalized for mental disorder than nonmigrants; and (4) the onset of some mental illnesses, especially schizophrenia, tends to be concentrated in the younger ages, the same ages at which migration is most prevalent.

Relationships between migration and mental health are undoubtedly highly complex. It is possible that it is not migration per se which leads to mental illness, but rather a combination of circumstances in conjunction with migration. Persons from relatively isolated rural areas migrating to large metropolitan centers, for example, may suffer from exposure to a new set of conditions which they are not prepared to meet. Receiving metropolitan areas often are not structured to provide easy

THOMAS R. PANKO

and rapid social adjustment to migrants from the hinterland. Extreme hostility, prejudice, discrimination, or even indifference on the part of the receiving community may be conducive to mental stress and strain. Southern Negroes or Appalachian whites moving to northern industrial centers are often confronted with segregation and discrimination in housing, employment, and other areas.

For some migrants, however, comparatively little change is involved in making a move; essentially the only change is their place of residence. For other migrants, moving to a new place with a new way of life and new opportunities may be a happy and healthy thing. It becomes important therefore to determine the conditions under which migration is associated with mental health as well as with mental illness.

Just as physical and mental handicaps serve as barriers to individuals in a myriad of ways, depending in part on their migrant-nonmigrant circumstances, other resource-mobilization combinations are related to the migrant status of individuals; for example, capability, motivation, personality, and socioeconomic status. The resulting poverty properties, as shown in Table 4.1, are not elaborated here. However, the complexities involved in the relationship can be illustrated further in the case of kinship bonds.

The kind and strength of kinship ties can be critical to the well-being of individuals whether they are migrants or not. But when it comes to questions of residential changes, especially those involving separations in conjunction with long-distance moves, family and kinship are often central concerns.

Where family ties are regarded as highly important, the sense of obligation and duty, the affection among family members, and the satisfaction derived from close and frequent contacts become crucial to decisions about migration and to subsequent adjustments to new communities. For example, among many Appalachian families, movement away from Appalachia interferes with and threatens to sever family and kinship bonds, and this is often perceived by the migrants themselves as the worst kind of "poverty." The absence of family members because of migration alters and often threatens the prior family structure and unity. In common parlance, a migrant may suffer from a severe case of homesickness.

Whereas revered, respected, and desired interactions with one's kin may tend to prevent moving away or contribute to great dissatisfaction and maladjustment for those who do migrate, already broken or mal-

TABLE 4.2   Poverty Properties at Points of Origin & Destination

Basic resources	Mobilization	Poverty properties
Natural resources	Technological development	Resources lacking, depleted or wasted
State policy	Programs Legislation Judicial process	Unmet needs "Welfare poor" Ineligibility for benefits
Economic system	Property rights Labor and capital Production, distribution and consumption	Lack of opportunity to own or control Obstacles to acquisition or exchange of goods and services High incidence of unemployment, low income and low levels of living
Social norms	Accessibility and acceptability	Norm deprivation Indifference or rebellion
Social stratification	Social mobility	High proportions of nonmobile and low status
Community services and facilities	Leadership and organization	Lack of leadership and organization Absence of services and facilities
Mass media	Dissemination of news and information	Uninformed citizenry

THOMAS R. PANKO

functioning family ties may be evaded by simply moving. In the case of a divorced migrant, resettlement may have the effect of leading to remarriage and the reestablishment of family life. The deserter can effectively avoid the stress and strain of an already malfunctioning home life. For the stayer, an unhappy family is his poverty.

Migration is a complex matter not only for individuals; it also has substantial effects on both sending and receiving communities. The poverty properties of communities or regions are especially important in a consideration of migration. A major concern is with differences between places of origin and destination, as suggested in Table 4.2. The columns listing resources, mobilization methods, and poverty properties are essentially identical to those presented in chapter 2. However, the perspective changes in a very important way as a result of the distinction between origin and destination. Hypothetically, a person might move from a place with specific poverty properties to a destination which would help reduce the magnitude of some of his own properties. There is always a danger for the individual mover that the result of moving is the replacement of some components of poverty by others.

Seen as either sending or receiving areas, communities tend to gain or lose, depending on the poverty traits of the communities and on the nature and extent of the properties of poverty among migrants. Among sending communities with high rates of unemployment, for instance, the outmigration of large numbers of unemployed helps to reduce unemployment problems. Sending communities with a labor shortage would tend to lose potential workers as a result of outmigration. As receiving areas, communities might also either increase or decrease their poverty properties depending on the nature of their problems in relation to the characteristics of incoming migrants.

Decisions to move and the movement of people between areas involves more than a simple comparison of advantages and disadvantages of the places of origin and destination. Between every two points there is a set of intervening obstacles (Lee 1966) or intervening opportunities (Stouffer 1940). As Lee points out, distance itself may be an obstacle, but there are also potential physical barriers and governmental policies. According to Lee's conception of intervening obstacles, positive and negative factors at origins and destinations are defined differently for every migrant. Stouffer, viewing the problem of obstacles in a positive way, formulated the hypothesis of intervening opportunities, according to which the flow of migrants between two places is inversely related to the number of opportunities between the two places for the migrants to satisfy their needs for such things as employment and housing. Stouffer's theory assumes that migration is costly and that a mobile person will cease moving as soon as he has satisfactory opportunities.

Despite some real difficulties in defining obstacles or opportunities empirically, these conceptions have potentially significant implications for people as migrants, for both sending and receiving communities, and for social service programs. Individual assessments of obstacles and opportunities are key factors in decisions to migrate, including the selection of a destination. Communities can develop in ways that either encourage or discourage migration; with the help of local, state, and national social service programs, they can help in controlling the selection and flow of people moving between different places, as well as in contributing to their adjustment.

How critical is the issue of migration, and how extensively does it affect communities? A brief discussion of migration in Appalachia can serve as an illustration of migration trends, patterns, and problems in a region widely characterized as poverty-stricken.

APPALACHIAN MIGRATION

A mass movement out of Appalachia has been going on for several decades. During the 1950s, this outmigration meant a numerical deficit exceeding one million people; in the 1960s net migration losses for the southern Appalachian area amounted to nearly 600,000 people. As population bases shrink in many localities, fewer potential migrants remain and the number of outmigrants may be expected to decrease. The loss of young adults through migration has been so great in some counties that the residual population is primarily composed of older adults. As a consequence, demographically and economically there is little basis for a regeneration of the population and economy.

The nonmetropolitan areas of Appalachia lose more heavily to migration than metropolitan areas. Over 80 percent of the net migration loss during the 1960s is accounted for by the losses in nonmetropolitan counties, as shown in Table 4.3. The average net migration loss for metropolitan counties was only 3.0 percent compared to a loss of 7.4 percent for nonmetropolitan counties. The nonmetropolitan counties of Kentucky and the Virginias suffered the heaviest losses in this

THOMAS R. PANKO

TABLE 4.3   Net Migration for Southern Appalachian Counties, 1960 to 1970

	Net migration (in thousands)			Net migration rate		
	Net change	Metro.	Non-metro.	Net change	Metro.	Non-metro.
All S. Appalachian counties	−592	−99	−493	− 6.1	− 3.0	− 7.4
Alabama	− 73	−33	− 41	− 3.7	− 2.9	− 4.7
Georgia	52	20	32	7.8	22.5	5.5
Kentucky	−147	− 5	−142	−15.9	− 9.5	−16.3
Maryland	− 2	- -	− 2	− 1.1	- -	− 1.1
Mississippi	− 35	- -	− 35	− 8.6	- -	− 8.6
North Carolina	− 4	4	− 8	− 0.5	1.1	− 1.4
South Carolina	− 4	9	− 12	− 0.6	3.4	− 3.8
Tennessee	− 46	−16	− 30	− 2.8	− 2.6	− 3.0
Virginia	− 74	- -	− 74	−14.8	- -	−14.8
West Virginia	−260	−78	−182	−13.9	−13.5	−14.1

Source: James S. Brown, "South Appalachian Population Change, 1960 to 1970" (Mimeographed, July, 1971).

Note: Figures apply to the 303 counties in Appalachia as defined by the Appalachian Regional Commission, excluding those of New York, Ohio, and Pennsylvania.

decade. Numerically, West Virginia counties lost the largest numbers through migration.

Much of the present movement of Appalachian people is similar to the movements of other migrants in this country. Appalachian residents tend to move short distances and to metropolitan or urban centers. Brown and Hillery (1962:63) found that, for 1949-50, migrants leaving the coal fields and hilly areas of Eastern Kentucky generally moved to Ohio, the destination being Cincinnati or Dayton. The attractions and opportunities in metropolitan areas, even in Appalachia, are suggested by the net gains of Georgia's metropolitan counties. Birmingham, Atlanta, and other metropolitan centers closely linked to Appalachia draw large numbers of migrants from nearby areas. The development of streams of migrants between particular points is not only a function of proximity, but also of relationships between settled migrants and their friends and relatives back home.

What factors have contributed to this massive migration in Appalachia? It is common knowledge that the economy of the Appalachian region is based on its coal reserves. "King Coal" has exerted a two-fold influence on the area. On the one hand, the mining of untold tons of coal has provided a livelihood for thousands of families. In its boom days coal was a dominant force in the settlement and growth of the area. However, the increased capital concentration by a few large companies has reduced the numbers of independent mining operations and their prospects for future growth.

Another factor prompting a continued decline in the Appalachian mining labor force relates to the preeminent position coal has occupied in this country's energy supply. Coal has been partially superseded by other forms of energy, such as gas, oil, and nuclear power. In addition, improved extractive techniques and automated procedures in the mining industry have displaced thousands of workers and created a large overflowing pool of reserve manpower. The continued decrease in employment possibilities in the region has served as a major stimulus for outmigration, as many workers seek jobs elsewhere. The magnitude of outmigration from Appalachia has just been documented. Since additional improvements in mining appear inevitable, migration should continue in the future, albeit at a reduced rate.

The continued outmigration of large numbers of people from Appalachia has created potentially serious problems for the region's future. Because migration is a selective process, a large proportion of those leaving the region are concentrated in the early age brackets, particularly between the ages of 20-29. Continued heavy outmigration of this age group has several consequences.

First, it means the loss of the community's most productive members in terms of years of possible employment. A somewhat nebulous benefit does accrue from outmigration in communities characterized by high rates of unemployment in that it reduces the number of unemployed. A frequent disadvantage for these Appalachian communities is that the unemployed who remain behind often lack the necessary skills for future employment and the community is not able to provide opportunities for vocational training. At destination sites, the influx of people seeking employment may aggravate existing situations. The implications for welfare programs are quite obvious.

The continued loss of young Appalachian adults also has an effect on the educational systems of sending and receiving communities. Since better educated Appalachian youths are more likely to migrate, their loss constitutes a drain on the educational reserves of the region and of their own communities. Further, because educational attainment is lower in Appalachia than in other parts of the country, the influx of migrants from that area tends to depress rates of educational attainment in the receiving communities.

Since the young outmigrants are also in the most productive child-bearing ages, their departure could reduce the fertility rates of the area. Moreover, continued heavy outmigration of this age group could mean that unless conditions improve in Appalachia these migrants and their children—future community leaders—will be lost forever to the area. The loss is cumulative; the outmigration of youth has the effect of "aging" the population in the sending area. Loss of the potentially most productive women (those with a large number of years of fertility risk) promotes population decline as a result of a top-heavy age pyramid.

Yet the ramifications of these occurrences are even more complex. With a greater total dependency ratio (the ratio of those in essentially the nonproductive years of under 15 and over 65 to the population in their productive years, 15 to 64), the tax burden of the community falls on fewer shoulders. This increased burden also may serve to promote continued outmigration and stifle the attraction of new business and industrial enterprises. With a smaller tax base, the possibility of supporting extensive, or even adequate, community services such as hospitals, health clinics, libraries, nursing homes, homes for the aged, school systems, recreation, and utilities becomes increasingly more difficult. Depopulation also results in decreased political representation. Consequently, it becomes more difficult to influence passage of ameliorative legislation.

A further consequence of this heavy outmigration could be increased psychic stress (as is evidenced on the vast and sparsely settled Great Plains area) in both sending and receiving communities.

In the sending community there may be a reduction in meaningful social interaction and peer group identification. And, although many Appalachian migrants move as family units to areas in which their relatives reside, adjustment to the new surroundings of the receiving community can still present certain types of psychological stresses and problems.

It is obvious that migration is a critical issue, not only posing problems on an individual level, but affecting communities as well. Further research efforts are essential if these problems are to be alleviated.

RESEARCH NEEDS

Migration is an intricate, dynamic process. The selective nature of migration involves a myriad of factors which affect both sending and receiving communities. In addition, migration contains problem-solving and problem-creating situations at individual, community, and national levels which have consequences for family structure, political and educational systems, health services, and occupational markets. Past efforts have shed some light on the nature and consequences of the redistribution of the Appalachian population. Yet, a considerable gap still remains between what is known and what needs to be known about this migration. The following recommendations are offered in the prospect of bridging this research gap.

An initial recommendation requires a reorientation of research perspectives. The ramifications stemming from migration dictate an interdisciplinary approach. As pointed out at a recent Southern Regional Education Board Conference (Panko 1969), one of the major weaknesses underlying current migration research is the tendency of investigators to view mobility solely within the conceptual framework of their particular discipline. Thus, sociologists, for example, have been concerned with the social aspects of migration, psychologists have focused

THOMAS R. PANKO

on various attitudinal and motivational dimensions, and economists have been interested in the economic consequences of migration. Although this type of approach is not without merit and does provide certain specific types of information, it necessarily leaves too many questions unanswered, too many issues unresolved. A more promising approach would involve the cooperation and coordination of efforts of students throughout the behavorial sciences. The results of studies conducted by such task forces then could be conveyed to persons in positions of authority capable of initiating and carrying through necessary remedial actions.

A second recommendation concerns migration adjustment. Some people are able to accomplish the transition to new surroundings with relative ease; for the greater proportion of Appalachian migrants, however, this transition often poses seemingly insurmountable obstacles. Indeed, much attention has been directed to the volume and flow of Appalachian migration but the problems individuals face and must cope with have been largely overlooked. Price (Panko 1969) has pointed out that there are a number of potentially useful indicators of migrant adjustment, one of the more obvious being financial self-sufficiency. Other indicators of adjustment, or maladjustment, include the proportion of migrants on welfare rolls; mean income of migrants as compared to income of the local nonmigrant population; percentage of migrants gainfully employed (a further refinement would be number of hours worked per week); duration of unemployment after a move; percentage of unemployed migrants; number of job changes made in a given period of time; participation in community organizations and political elections; frequency of return visits home; number of new friends in receiving locale. More attention should be directed to exploring these indicators of adjustment and uncovering others which may exist. For example, consideration should be given to identifying the factors underlying and promoting the higher rates of delinquency, mental illness, family disorganization, and school absenteeism found among migrants.

A third recommendation focuses on migration data sources and data analytical techniques. Nineteen-forty marked the first time the census included a question on migration during a fixed time interval. By asking the respondent his place of residence in 1935, a determination could be made of his "migration status," that is, whether he was still living in the same place or not. Most of the data employed in studying internal migration in the United States has come from this source; it has been of inestimable value. To complement and extend the information available in census materials, additional techniques can be employed.

In a paper presented at the International Population Conference in Vienna, Price (1965) suggested increased utilization of computer facilities to simulate social behavior. Specifically, Price reported that progress is being made on the development of an internal migration model using probability techniques and electronic data processing capabilities. The initial problem of assigning to an individual a probability of moving across a state boundary in a given time period can be solved on the basis of certain selected characteristics such as age, sex, race, and marital status. This information, "plugged" into the migration model and processed by computer, yields probabilities which can be used as predictors of the mobility of given segments of a population residing in a specified area at a certain time. The use of this technique could present sending and receiving communities with an opportunity to plan for long-range adjustment.

Another promising development is the increased recognition of the value of longitudinal studies of migration. In longitudinal studies, migration is considered in the context of the total life of the individual. Three examples of this approach are found in recent articles by Wilber, Eldridge, and Shryock and Larmon; they are presented here in capsule form.

Applying probability techniques to hypothetical cohorts, Wilber (1963) was able to derive estimates of the total lifetime mobility (TLM) which an average individual would experience. Calculation of total lifetime mobility rates is relatively straightforward and directly analogous to that for determining net reproductive rates. Since age-specific migration rates can be treated as independent probabilities, the TLM is simply the summation of these probabilities across all ages, with an allowance for survivorship included in the computational formula. The results of these calculations indicate that in his lifetime the average individual will migrate four times and change his place of residence thirteen times. The logic underlying this approach is that the migration experience of one cohort may differ markedly from that of other cohorts depending on prevailing social, economic, historical, and political conditions. The possibilities of this approach include detecting trends, making comparisons, and exacting more precise migration data.

Eldridge (1964) employed a longitudinal cohort approach to determine the possible association between migration rates and economic

THOMAS R. PANKO

fluctuations. In an initial step she delineated two cohorts on the basis of economic conditions that prevail during the decade in which they were 25-29 years old. For one cohort passing through these years there was relative prosperity; the other cohort experienced a recession. While usual procedures for correlating time series of economic activity and migration rates provided inconsistent results and inadequate explanations, these problems were resolved in the cohort approach. Eldridge found that migration rates were higher in the "prosperity cohort" and peaked at earlier ages. Her conclusion was that age-specific migration rates are affected by economic conditions.

Shryock and Larmon (1965) have argued rather convincingly for combining longitudinal and life history data. They point out that migration measures are inherently longitudinal since such measures involve a comparison of residence at two different points in time. If life history data are incorporated with longitudinal data it is possible to determine the association between changes in mobility and changes in other statuses such as employment, fertility, and income. Moreover, this approach makes possible the sequencing of these events.

The resource-mobilization framework provides a mechanism to (1) help synthesize much of existing research and (2) examine the multitudinous relations between the independence and well-being of individuals and regions and the phenomena of migration. Specific studies, for example, might investigate relationships among the health, socioeconomic status, and kinship resources of individuals and, in turn, how these personal resources are modified by the use of community services and facilities, educational attainment, employment, occupational level, income, and family organization (or disorganization). Within the community (or regional) context, there are critically important questions relating to the impact of migrant flows on sending and receiving areas. Although it is evident people tend to move from less attractive to more attractive locations, the precise role of the nature and degree of "attractiveness" in influencing such moves is not yet clear. Neither is it clear that the loss, for example, of low income persons through migration has the effect of elevating the sending community's resources and depressing the receiving area's resources. It is also uncertain how specific types and levels of services and facilities influence people to move or stay and what kind of change in social services would be required for effective discouragement (or encouragement) of migration.

In sum, these recommendations have been offered from the standpoint that, although current data sources and analytical techniques are adequate for certain purposes, alternative strategies should be considered. Improved research designs and sharper methodological tools can yield more precise insights into the motivations prompting migration, the adjustment of migrants to new surroundings, and the consequences of migration. The results of these insights and refinements will lead, it is to be hoped, to the development of cause and effect models and a general theory of migration.

5 Social Services for Migrants

Thomas R. Panko

A basic freedom in this country is the ability of any person to move whenever, wherever, and as often as he chooses. That we are indeed a highly mobile nation is evidenced by the fact that each year one in every five persons changes his place of residence. Mobility, however, entails much more than the movement of people from one location to another. As indicated in chapter 4, these changes in the population can, and often do, affect the social organization and value systems of communities, political and educational systems, occupational markets, family structure, and city planning.

Yet, despite the many possible consequences of migration, we do not have a policy to control movement in the United States nor a national program of assistance for those who do move. At the present time, there is a paucity of services available to migrants and, further, current programs are geared to certain segments of the migrant population only. Initial discussion will be focused on the types of programs and assistance now in effect. These programs are located at the national, state, and local levels and will be treated in that sequence.

SERVICES FOR INTERNATIONAL MIGRANTS

There are in existence several United States government programs which offer assistance and services to international (as opposed to internal) migrants and refugees (Brody 1969). Perhaps the most notable example is the Cuban Refugee Program. The major emphasis of this program involves the relocation of Cuban refugees in areas outside Miami. This is accomplished by providing migrants with one-way tickets to their choice of destination. Other direct benefits and services are provided in the form of emergency financial assistance to certain eligible refugees, providing for medical care, adult education programs, and, in some cases, housing. Direct allocations are also made to the city of Miami and surrounding environs to alleviate the impact of any large influx of refugees. The Office of Refugee and Migration Affairs also operates several programs offering assistance to refugees from various parts of the world, providing educational facilities, medical services, vocational training, and resettlement assistance.

Many voluntary private agencies offer assistance and services to immigrants. For example, American ORT (Organization for Rehabilitation through Training Federation) operates a vocational school in New York City primarily for Jewish refugees, offering vocational and technical training for adults, vocational training for youth, apprentice placement for on-the-job training, and aid in finding employment.

Other private agencies offering aid to immigrants include the American Council for Emigrés in the Professions, Inc., specializing in counseling and placement services, and the American Council for Nationalities Services, which emphasizes services to, and resettlement of, refugees and immigrants to the United States.

SERVICES FOR INTERNAL MIGRANTS

In marked contrast to the number of programs designed to assist immigrants from other countries to the United States is the apparent lack of large-scale organized assistance and services to migrants within the country. While there are some programs which offer services to various categories of migrants—for example, assistance to migrant agricultural workers—the migrant population as a whole seems to be a rather neglected group.

Federal programs designed specifically for migratory agricultural workers and their families are aimed at a variety of specific problems. The goal of the Educationally Deprived Children Program is to identify and meet the special needs of migrant children through remedial instruction, health, nutritional, and psychological services, cultural development, and pre-vocational training and counseling. Another example is

THOMAS R. PANKO

that of the Handicapped Migratory Workers Program, which operates pilot projects for rehabilitative services.

The Migrant Health Grants Program seeks to elevate the health status of migratory farm workers and their families to national norms by providing comprehensive health services (medical, nursing, dental, health education, hospitalization, and sanitation). A corollary project is the Migrant Health Technical Assistance Program, the focus of which is the improvement of health services available to migrant farm workers and the integration of these services into a comprehensive health care system especially for rural communities.

Another project, sponsored by the Office of Economic Opportunity, is the Migrant and Seasonal Farm Workers Assistance Program, which offers assistance in the form of day care, education and rehabilitation, health services, improved housing and sanitation, consumer education, and counseling. In addition, long-term programs are designed to increase community acceptance of migrants and to assist them in adapting to the changing demands of an increasingly technological society. Many of the services offered by these programs to migratory farm workers are, in fact, needed by many other categories of migrants.

For financially needy migrants who meet the other eligibility requirements for public welfare, there is now a possibility of assistance under the federal-state public assistance programs. Examples of these are: Aid to the Blind, Old Age Assistance, Aid to the Permanently and Totally Disabled, and Aid to Families with Dependent Children.

Until quite recently, migrants were systematically excluded from these programs because they couldn't meet the residence requirements for eligibility. As late as 1967, forty jurisdictions maintained residential requirements of one year immediately preceding application for AFDC. Approximately the same number of jurisdictions had residency requirements ranging from one year to five of the last nine years, with one year continuous residence immediately preceding application. These residency requirements were declared unconstitutional by the U.S. Supreme Court decision in *Shapiro* v. *Thompson* (1969). However, welfare programs reflecting various types of assistance and services continue to be confined to certain categories of needy persons.

In addition to financial assistance, welfare recipients (including qualified migrants) are provided with supportive social services. Generally, these services include case work, group work, family counseling, information and referral services, protective services, child care, legal services, family planning, home and money management, and consumer education. The emphasis of these services is on self-help, rehabilitation, and strengthening of family life. Welfare recipients are also entitled to a variety of medical services under the Medicaid Program including in-patient and out-patient care, skilled nursing home services, lab and X-ray services, and physicians' services. Persons who do not qualify for welfare but are classified as "medically needy" are also eligible for these forms of medical assistance in several states.

Finally, various manpower services are available to welfare recipients who are participants in the Work Incentive Program (WIN); included are on-the-job training, basic education, skill training, work orientation, work experience, and follow-through supportive services to improve employability.

For needy migrants who do not fall into any of the categories eligible for the public welfare programs, there is the possibility of "emergency assistance" in several states as an optional part of the state welfare program. Emergency assistance is extended in specific situations (e.g., loss of utility services, exhaustion of food supplies). In the form of financial aid, medical care, or services, it may be made available to migrants throughout the state or in certain specified areas for a maximum period of thirty days per year. In addition, the states offer "general assistance," covering needy persons who fail to qualify for the federal-state categorical assistance programs; these tend to be limited in scope, however.

The various labor mobility demonstration projects (created in 1963 as the result of amendments to the Manpower Development and Training Act of 1962) also offer financial and nonfinancial assistance and services to certain groups of migrants participating in these projects. Eligibility is limited to persons who are involuntarily unemployed without local prospects for suitable employment and to members of low income farm families. These projects assist the relocation of unemployed persons and attempt to increase the migration from rural areas to centers of economic activity. In a sense, these programs provide a mechanism for alleviating structural unemployment resulting from changes in the location and composition of economic activity; they also constitute a form of assisted migration (Fairchild 1970:5).

One service offered through these demonstration projects is the collection and distribution of information concerning job openings (on a regional basis) through the Interarea Clearance System. This service has as its goal the matching of workers with jobs in demand areas. Additional detailed information is provided, such as directions for reaching demand area and where to report upon arrival. In some cases, provisions are made for preemployment interview trips (Fairchild 1970:75-84).

Further, these projects include assistance in the form of relocating the worker in his new community, providing information on transportation facilities, and giving advice on health care, legal matters, educational facilities, and pre-move preparations. The labor mobility demonstration projects vary in their capacity to provide these services. The most successful approach has been by contract with the Travelers Aid Association of America. Several projects found this private organization to provide more-than-adequate supportive services in the supply and demand areas (Fairchild 1970:88). Unfortunately, Travelers Aid is an organization located predominantly in large urban centers and is apparently unknown to the bulk of migrants.

Labor mobility demonstration projects provide valuable services to certain classes of migrants, that is, to those who are participants in relocation programs. Since these services are offered on a limited basis to a particular group of people, they are not part of a national program. The services they do offer are needed by—and ideally should be furnished to—all migrants who require them. However, lacking such a national program, migrants must continue to rely on their personal resources or on their knowledge of private organizations offering assistance.

One such private organization is the Urban League, which assists migrants in urban areas. With branches located in more than sixty cities, the Urban League constantly strives to promote more cooperation and understanding between whites and Negroes. In recent years, the League has become increasingly active in seeking solutions to the problems encountered by great numbers of rural southern Negroes migrating to large industrial centers (Myers 1959:90). A concerted effort has been directed to the problems of adjustment which these migrants face in their new surroundings. In effect, they have moved from a traditional cultural setting to a highly industrialized and demanding cultural milieu, where their problems of adjustment are often manifested in high delinquency and crime rates, mental disorders, marital dissolution, and concomitant family disorganization. The League also tries to help families in crisis and emergency situations. Thus, while primarily assisting urban Negroes rather than migrants per se, the League in the course of its activities does provide valuable services to one major category of migrants.

Various local private and civic organizations have been established with the express purpose of assisting migrants in adapting to their new environment. Welcome Wagon is an example of such an organization. The major objective of Welcome Wagon is to distribute city maps, literature describing the area, gift certificates, and special introductory offers redeemable at local businesses. Newcomer clubs are another example of local organizations which send representatives to greet those newly arrived. These clubs are organized primarily for social reasons. After initial contact has been made, newcomers are invited to attend meetings held at the homes of other recent newcomers to the area. In addition to visiting and making acquaintances, the new recruit is invited to participate in such activities as card playing and handicrafts.

Some communities have inaugurated programs expressly designed to assist and deliver supportive social services to Appalachian migrants. One of these organizations is Hub Services, Inc., a nonprofit corporation established as part of the Cincinnati Model Cities Program. Hub estimates there are between 50,000 to 100,000 unassimilated Appalachian migrants in the Cincinnati area alone (Branscome 1971:4-8). Providing comprehensive services to these migrants encourages assimilation and mitigates the impact on the city. Also assisting Appalachian migrants is an organization known as FOCI (The Federation of Communities in Service to Appalachia). FOCI services include recreational programs designed to alleviate the unhappiness characteristic of many Appalachian children who have been transplanted to large urban centers.

Religion, too, is an important facet of Appalachian and southern culture. Realizing this, religious organizations in various cities throughout the country have established programs to help these immigrants. One such program is carried out under the auspices of the Methodist church at Cincinnati's Emmanuel Community Center (Freedman and Wagner 1965:320). The primary objective of the program is to help incoming Negroes and southern mountain people establish meaningful relationships in their new surroundings. Recreational, social, and educational services are provided in a daily group work program for nearly a thousand people. A day care center supplying supervision of children for approximately fifty working women, a casework program for needy families, and an orientation program for newcomers to Cincinnati are

THOMAS R. PANKO

activities included in this program (Freedman and Wagner 1965:321).

The Southern California Council of Churches, located in Los Angeles, also has recognized the need to provide supportive services to inner-city youth, since Los Angeles continually receives large numbers of migrants from the rural South. Employing a method similar to many Big Brother programs throughout the nation, this organization provides for children of newly arrived families to receive counseling from individual laymen. In their close relationship the layman attempts to see the city through the boy's eyes and help him deal realistically with any adjustment problems (Freedman and Wagner 1965:321).

Several programs have been established in the nation's larger urban centers to handle the problems of rural youth immigrants. The two significant indicators of the success with which these rural youth will adapt to their environments are education and employment. "Education transmits the skills and provides motivation for 'making it' in the receiving society. Employment in a meaningful occupation with adequate financial rewards is, in our society, a test of whether in fact a person has 'made it' " (Freedman and Wagner 1965:311). One institution that ought to be able to reach young rural migrants and help with adjustment problems is the public school system; but too often the schools are merely overwhelmed with the problems and offer little real assistance.

Milwaukee is one city which has translated into an active effort its concern for the successful adjustment of incoming rural youth. In 1961, the city initiated a special series of ungraded classes to serve as a reception center for children just entering the area from places outside the state, particularly the South. This arrangement is also available to city youth who are members of highly transient families, that is, those who constantly move from one neighborhood to another. To facilitate the adjustments these youths must make, special classes with a maximum enrollment of twenty students have been introduced at elementary, junior high, and high school levels. The thrust of this plan is the provision of social, psychological, and curriculum services through individualized attention. An outstanding feature of the Milwaukee program is that students may enter these special classes at any time during the year. This is a highly realistic approach since a family may move at any time, regardless of the school calendar. Under this arrangement, students are admitted into the regular Milwaukee school program as soon as they have demonstrated the skills required for their grade.

One elementary school in Chicago has a large enrollment of children from Eastern Kentucky and West Virginia. Nearly three-fourths of these children transferred in or out of school as many as three and four times in a single year (Freedman and Wagner 1965:323). To cope with the educational transiency of these migrant children, the school's officials have devised an ingenious plan. The first step is an orientation program to determine the child's grade level. After this decision has been reached a "pal" of his own age is assigned to help him in adjustment. Coincident with these efforts are attempts to discourage parents from making unnecessary moves which interrupt their children's education (Myers 1959). Establishment of educational programs similar to those operative in Milwaukee and Chicago is recommended as an integral part of a national migrant policy.

Another type of program oriented to youth development has been proposed by an organization known as Action for Appalachian Youth, focusing on Kanawha County in West Virginia. Kanawha County's youth left the area in large numbers in the period 1950-60. This outmigration amounted to approximately one-fourth the males 15-19 years of age, and one-third of the males 20-24 years old. Realizing that continued migration on this scale would constitute a serious drain on one of the area's most valuable assets—future leaders—Action for Appalachian Youth proposed a demonstration project. This project, known as KEY (Kanawha Employment for Youth), focused on lack of employment opportunities, a major motivation for outmigration of the county's youth. In 1962, nearly 7,000 youth in the county sought employment; this figure was expected to reach 9,000 by 1967 (Freedman and Wagner 1965:315-16). Often employment is not readily available, and Kanawha's youth leave to find work in other parts of the country. However, since many of these youth are poorly equipped occupationally, they have found a comparable lack of employment in other areas. Consequently they tend to return to Kanawha. This county's disadvantaged youth needs occupational training as well as various kinds of help in their adjustment to urban life. KEY was developed precisely to meet these needs.

The problems which KEY is attempting to solve are characteristic of other rural Appalachian areas and, thus, a close examination of the program's techniques is warranted. An initial problem involves delivering their services to Kanawha's youth since the county is highly rural and most of the families live in isolated hollows. Realizing the logistics

　　　　　　　　　　　　　　　THOMAS R. PANKO

of the situation, KEY proposes to contact these youth at the places where they live.

Caring little about formal education, Kanawha's youth find it difficult to function in a school setting. Accordingly, KEY intends to establish centers offering job skills in a rural outdoor setting. Further, Kanawha's disadvantaged youth will be allowed to study under craftsmen who are sympathetic and understanding of their situation rather than under traditional teachers with whom they find it so hard to identify. These craftsmen will provide the necessary skills for future employability as well as the advice and counsel needed by the youth. Since the traditional Appalachian culture includes suspicion of strangers, this represents a realistic approach.

Another realistic aspect of the KEY program is the type of training to be provided. The task of providing locally the skills necessary for employment in the chemical industry, which predominates in the Kanawha Valley, is almost insurmountable. Therefore, an on-the-job training program outside the state is being contemplated. Columbus, Ohio represents such a site since many of Kanawha's youth seek employment there. Providing a training facility in Columbus would serve a dual purpose: it would provide skills transportable to the home community and would furnish an opportunity for these Appalachian youth to adapt to urban conditions (Freedman and Wagner 1965:315-17).

A NATIONAL MIGRATION POLICY

Most migrant assistance programs are designed for particular categories of migrants. Services tend to be confined to meeting specific needs. Thus, the general migrant population seems to have been neglected and the need for a more encompassing migration policy seems obvious. For such a policy to be successful, however, consideration must be directed to the assistance efforts in communities of origin as well as in the receiving communities. Under most current programs, migrants are eligible for assistance only after they have moved—the burden of program initiation and delivery resting with the host community. Some viable policy guidelines at local, regional, and national levels are suggested by three recent studies.

As an integral component of migration policy, the first study suggests the possibility of establishing communication centers similar to the one proposed by the East Tennessee Development District (*Appalachia* 1970:16-22). The central office would be in Jacksboro, but neighborhood service workers would be available in each of the surrounding ten rural counties. Such availability is an all-important "ingredient" in any policy concerned with providing services to rural residents. Frequently a community may possess facilities and services which are unknown to residents of outlying areas. This situation may arise because telephones or transportation are lacking or because people are too timorous to inquire about such services. The Communication Center could provide a solution to this problem since it would convey relevant information to people at convenient locations.

The Center would transmit at least three types of information. First, it would make known existing services and programs available in the area and tell how and where to apply for them. Second, it would provide information on employment opportunities in the area's growth centers. In addition to maintaining a list of job openings, the Center would furnish medical, educational, and housing information. Finally, arrangements would be made to channel suggestions of area residents to officials at all governmental levels. The program's feedback aspect accomplishes two objectives: (1) it brings to the fore what many programs lack—local community involvement, and (2) it furnishes a means for conveying the needs of people in the area to those in positions of authority. The East Tennessee Development Program is an example of the type of effort that can be made at the local level.

A study conducted for the Office of Economic Opportunity has major implications for migration policy. It deals with three specific migration streams: (1) the stream of southeastern blacks from Virginia, Georgia, and the Carolinas whose primary destinations are northeastern metropolitan areas; (2) the stream of Spanish-Americans migrating from the rural areas of Colorado and New Mexico to metropolitan centers in that area and on the Pacific Coast; and (3) the stream of Appalachian white migrants leaving the rural areas of Kentucky and West Virginia for cities in Ohio (*Appalachia* 1971:9-10). The specific purposes of the study were twofold: to determine the probable causes of migration and to provide information on the migration process per se. The study was not explicitly designed to determine whether a regional (or national) policy to reduce and redirect migration should be advocated. However, if that possibility arises, findings of this study could be translated into the following policy strategies:

THOMAS R. PANKO

1. To prevent a further drain on the region's human resources (i.e., its people), economic shocks which encourage outmigration can be diminished if steady and accessible jobs are available.

2. Secondary to the provision of job opportunities should be the improvement of services (e.g., more adequate housing, improved quality of educational systems, etc.).

3. Increased possibility of land and home ownership and greater opportunity for community involvement through self-help programs are two possible means of curbing migration since it can be assumed that if an individual's ties to an area are increased this may serve as a deterrent to migration.

4. A migration policy should include increased and improved transportation capabilities to cope with the isolation of workers from their jobs and existing services. Potential obstacles to migration are lack of finances for purchasing personal means of transportation and/or the inaccessibility of public modes of transportation.

5. Increased benefits to those not in the labor force, including the elderly and the indigent, can also be a deterrent to outmigration; these benefits could be implemented through a comprehensive family assistance program.

6. A more urban atmosphere to hold youth within the area would be created; this would include a wider range of civic and recreational services to increase the chance for participation in the community and bring the community in closer harmony with the larger society.

The author suggests that these strategies may effect a reduction in the rate of rural to urban migration and thus stimulate the growth of smaller regional centers in areas such as Appalachia.

A more comprehensive program has been recommended by the President's National Advisory Commission on Rural Poverty. Five recommendations of the Commission bear reporting here (*The People Left Behind* 1967:30-31):

1. All employment service offices actively collect and maintain current lists of labor market vacancies in the public and private sectors of their immediate areas; these vacancies should be filed with the employment service offices by officials at all governmental levels.

2. All employment service offices should actively collect and maintain lists of persons available for employment in their respective labor market area; special emphasis here is focused on registering the area's unemployed and disadvantaged workers.

SOCIAL SERVICES FOR MIGRANTS

3. Regular surveys of rural labor market conditions should be undertaken by the appropriate government agencies to provide an accurate picture of employment trends.

4. Annual plans for providing employment and training opportunities should be submitted by local employment offices in their respective areas.

5. Finally, as a part of its duties the U.S. Employment Service System should establish a nationwide computer service for matching employment opportunities with applicants available for work.

In addition to providing employment information in supply and demand areas, an internal migration policy should include services in noneconomic areas. Some of these services (e.g., health counseling and legal advice) are incorporated in current programs designed for specific migrant populations. Although the following list of services is not exhaustive of those needed by migrants, they are considered essential to any future migration policy. These programs should provide information on the location and availability of various public services, information concerning laws and statutes which may differ from those found at the community of origin, comprehensive listings of available housing, assistance in locating such housing, language courses to help migrants who do not speak standard English (particularly relevant for many Appalachian youth), meetings with local personnel officers, and migrant counseling.

In sum, there is little doubt that migration can be a stressful situation. For many Appalachian migrants successful adjustment to new surroundings is closely related to whether they have relatives in the new community, even though in some instances deep familiar involvement may mean the perpetuation of the mountain value system. Other migrants, lacking contacts in the area of destination, often suffer "migration shock." This testifies to the pressing need for community-integrating mechanisms and institutions; it also points up the need for some type of migration policy.

Implicit throughout the discussion of the many aspects of migration is the interdisciplinary nature of research on the topic. Extending our understanding of this important component of social change requires cooperation and coordination of efforts. Establishing a migration policy within an interdisciplinary framework can do much to ameliorate problems associated with migration.

THOMAS R. PANKO

RESEARCH NEEDS

Much of the evidence indicating that people who migrate need services and assistance is intuitive and impressionistic. For policy purposes there is a strikingly obvious gap in information about needs in relation to migration. If national policy concerning migration of people within the United States is in essence "no policy," and if this is to remain the status quo, there should be little cause for concern about the needs of migrants. On the other hand, if there is a serious concern for meeting real needs for services and assistance, then policy decision should be based on the best information available.

The lack of concrete data concerning migrant needs can be attributed, in part, to an orientation dominating many mobility studies. In this orientation migration is viewed in ex post facto fashion; concern is focused on migration after it has occurred. Typical results of these studies are expressed in terms of the number of people who have left an area and their place of destination. This approach implies migration is a static phenomenon—that it can be lifted out of its temporal and situational contexts for analytical purposes. Since such studies circumvent the behavorial dimensions inherent in migration, recommendations for assisting migrants in their relocation in new surroundings are generally nonexistent. As long as a static approach to the study of migration predominates, a realistic evaluation may be that we are missing the "big picture."

A more promising approach advocated at a 1969 conference (Research in Adaptation of Migrants) treats migration in dynamic terms, that is, as an ongoing process. There it was pointed out that, in addition to reporting areas of gain or loss, researchers should also seek answers to the following kinds of questions: What are the motivations prompting the decision to move? How does the migration process affect the individual and his family? What kind of problems does the migrant encounter upon arrival in a new community? What types of services or programs can he take advantage of to facilitate his adjustment to a new environment? What are the implications or consequences of migration on the institutional structures in the areas of origin and destination?

At this point, results of migration studies do not answer their questions. The truth is that almost nothing is known about the needs of potential or recent migrants. Even those who argue most vigorously that people with needs should receive help seem unaware that migrants, too, may have needs that go unsatisfied. Often the argument is advanced that migrants are not a unique group and are eligible to receive the same services as others. Unfortunately, the reality of migration and its aftermath suggests that adjustment problems may reach crisis proportions.

Whether the need for migrant services is a "straw man" or a reality can be determined by extensive study. How many people can be identified as potential migrants at any given time? How many of these actually move within a relatively short time? To what extent do they need premigration help in such matters as information on which to base the decision to move, the procurement of employment and housing, the location of health and legal services at the destination, the placement of children in schools, and even the securing of job training and employment counseling? Similarly, to what extent do migrants need assistance during and immediately after the process of changing residential location? Hard data required to answer such questions simply do not exist. Efforts are being made to determine the need for family planning services, as indicated in chapter 7, but no comparable attempt has been made to meet this need for migrants.

Estimating the needs of migrants is a very difficult task, and this may explain why there have been so few attempts thus far. For example, the task of defining needs is itself difficult to handle in any generally satisfactory manner; yet enough is known about subjectively perceived (as opposed to objectively determined) standards to make a start in this direction. Although migrants may have multiple needs, this does not mean the problem is unmanageable. At the risk of oversimplifying, one could begin with such needs as public assistance, health, housing, education, job training, employment service, and legal aid. The methodological, data gathering, and organizing tasks appear formidable. However, the presence of such difficulties is not sufficient reason to ignore the unmet needs of migrants, or, indeed, to ignore what may be a relatively great national problem.

6 Appalachian Fertility

George L. Wilber

High rates of fertility have prevailed for centuries among economically depressed peoples. The fear of the economic effects of excessive fertility and overpopulation has gradually become widespread. And, correctly or not, many people associate large populations with political, social and environmental problems. The prospect of controlling fertility and population growth has become an economic and technological reality; many countries already are moving toward fertility control.

Fertility is viewed by some as an entirely demographic phenomenon—as one of the three components of population growth; and, in this sense, fertility is related not only to growth, but to the distribution and composition of a population. The focus of this chapter, however, will be on childbearing. Relationships between childbearing and family planning are important since family planning can serve several purposes: to control population growth, to protect and improve health, to liberate women, and to reduce the burdens of impoverished people. Family planning services will be examined in the following chapter. Of chief concern in this chapter will be the effects of family planning on poverty. If fertility can be effectively controlled in regions, cities, and rural areas, not only economic but other aspects of poverty should be mitigated. For individuals and families, fertility control should mean improved opportunities to reduce one or more dimensions of poverty.

For example, large families have been traditional in rural Appalachia, especially in low income and relatively isolated areas. While present evidence indicates that fertility rates are declining in Appalachia, it is not clear that the poorest families are having proportionately fewer children, and, if so, whether having fewer children is alleviating the families' burdens when it comes to food, shelter, and clothing.

Out of the vast literature on fertility, the following discussion concentrates on only a few of the more relevant considerations: theoretical issues via demographic transition theory and fertility as a poverty component, fertility trends and differentials in the United States and Appalachia, infant and maternal mortality, implications of fertility for the Appalachian poor, and needed research.

SOME THEORETICAL ISSUES

Demographic transition theory, in essence, says that nations or areas of the world can be classified into three categories in accordance with fertility and mortality rates (Peterson 1969). Populations move through three growth stages. The first stage is characterized by high fertility rates and high, but fluctuating, mortality rates which result in either a static population or a low rate of growth. Population growth is essentially uncontrolled. The second stage, called the Early Western, represents a continuation of high levels of fertility while mortality comes under control and death rates decline. Rapid growth—a population explosion—marks the second stage. The Modern Western, or third stage, is characterized by a generally slow growth of population which typically results from controlled and relatively low rates of fertility and mortality. In the process of transition, societies presumably move from a primitive, agricultural type of economy to an urban-industrial economy at the third stage.

There are at least two elaborations of the demographic transition theory which propose refinements. First, Cowgill (1963) argues that a systematic statement of the theory should include not only birth and death trends but also such variables as changes in size and form of the family, differential fertility and mortality, differential sex ratios, the aging of the population, and shifts to urban-industrial occupations and urban residence. These intermediate demographic variables are potentially important in any effort to explain population growth patterns. In addition, Cowgill suggests three very general kinds of variables—technology, culture, and attitudes—that need to be included in a theoretical model if it is to be of value in explaining population trends.

GEORGE L. WILBER

A second extension of demographic theory is proposed by Freedman (1965), who advocates a broad and bold approach to the study of fertility which would include the whole array of social and demographic variables. In this way we can study variation over time and link them into chains of influence for individuals, groups, regions, and countries. Freedman cites four broad groups of variables: (1) period and cohort measures of fertility in major population strata; (2) intermediate demographic variables through which social variables must operate to affect fertility; (3) social norms relevant to the intermediate variables; and (4) the elements of social and economic organization which affect the norms, the intermediate variables, and ultimate fertility. Freedman's scheme offers a framework not only for the analysis of fertility but also for migration, population growth, and other changes. Note that the direction of influence runs from organization through norms to the intermediate variables which exert a direct influence on fertility.

One of the most obvious extensions of transition theory involves the addition of migration as a third component of population growth. A complete theory of demographic transition might begin by taking population growth as the dependent variable. Growth is directly dependent on fertility, migration, and mortality. If each of these three components were dichotomized as high and low, eight possible kinds of combinations result.

Fertility, migration, and mortality—the growth components—not only influence population growth directly but are susceptible to similar influences. Various aspects of the family and of socioeconomic status, for example, are related to all three components although not necessarily in the same way. High socioeconomic status and a nuclear family structure are conducive to low fertility rates, low death rates, and possibly to relatively low rates of migration to other regions. Social norms may be more or less directly relevant to fertility, family planning, and other service programs as well as to various aspects of social and economic organization. In addition to the norms, various aspects of social and economic organization may exert influences on fertility. School systems, churches, the mass media, and social service organizations are examples of influential organizations. The kind and level of technology in an area and the rate of technological change also need to be incorporated into demographic transition theory. In general, where modern technology has been developed the furthest, urban-industrial organizational development is likely to be the most advanced. There is as much need to take into account the influence of technological factors pertinent to population growth or the control of births as to economic production.

On a purely impressionistic basis, Appalachia would appear to be somewhere in the transition process with declining fertility and mortality and continuing heavy outmigration. For both theoretical and program purposes, the nature and extent of a demographic transition in Appalachia requires careful examination. This has not been done in any comprehensive, systematic way. If the theoretical model should hold for Appalachia, it would provide a basis for prediction of future fertility. Such a model would also be useful for policy formulation, planning, and programming.

To return to the strategy of chapter 2, we may treat as a property of poverty the bearing of closely spaced and numerous children. Standards for defining too frequent or numerous births must be arbitrary, at least for the moment, but there is a widespread tendency to associate economic poverty with high fertility. The title of Rainwater's book *And the Poor Get Children* sums up what most people know or believe. Numerous studies support the proposition that fertility and income are inversely related. Implied in the concept of the cycle of poverty is the notion that the poor have children because they are poor and continue to be poor because they have too many children. As noted previously, demographic transition theory suggests that populations progressing toward lower and controlled natality rates are also becoming urban-industrial and more economically prosperous.

As a property of poverty, childbearing may be considered as a function of resources and resource mobilization. Tables 6.l and 6.2 sketch ways in which fertility and closely related phenomena, such as infant and maternal deaths, fit the general scheme of analysis. For areas or communities, the primary resource behind natality (at least from a demographic view) is the population of the area—its size, composition, and distribution. The degree to which health services in general and family planning services in particular are utilized effectively to control births and infant and maternal mortality illustrates mobilization of resources. In addition to population resources and their mobilization for fertility and infant and maternal mortality, all of the resources for areas and individuals are potentially related to childbearing. State policy, for example, became a relevant determinant of fertility in the United States during the 1960s, as indicated in the next chapter.

GEORGE L. WILBER

TABLE 6.1   Fertility & Fertility-related Poverty Properties
of Individuals

Resource	Mobilization	Poverty property
Health	Use of health and family planning facilities and services	Failure to use, ineffectiveness of or inaccessibility of services
Capability	Knowledge and skill to control fertility	Inability to control childbearing
Motivation	Acceptance and practice of family planning Family-size ideals	Family formation goal absent, unrealistic, or blocked
Personality	Socialization for fertility control	Immaturity, indifference re family formation
Socioeconomic status	Education and income adequate for effective fertility control	Lack of status achievement combined with lack of childbearing control

At the individual level, childbearing is a function of individual resources and their mobilization in the same fundamental way as for other properties of poverty. In this instance, however, "too many" is a poverty trait, in contrast with "too little" of something else, such as income. Measurement of natality through one or another of various rates is sufficiently developed for most research purposes, and the counting of births is generally simple and reliable. In terms of a poverty threshold, there is no generally accepted standard for a high birth rate or for too many births per mother. The same is true for infant and maternal deaths and for the spacing and timing of births. This may be fortunate for research purposes since fertility and closely related phenomena can be treated as a continuous variable. However, for policy and program purposes the establishment of thresholds can be useful. Unless some particular standard, such as Zero Population Growth, is accepted, there is no easy way to define "too much."

TABLE 6.2   Fertility & Fertility-related Poverty Properties for Areas & Collectivities

Resources	Mobilization	Poverty property
Population size, composition, and distribution	Population control	
Natural resources	Technology to facilitate fertility control	
State policy	Policy, planning and program for control of childbearing	
Economic system	Manufacture and distribution of birth control products	High rates of fertility and maternal and infant mortality
Social norms	Family size Maternal and child care	
Stratification	Social mobility	
Community services and facilities	Health and family planning	
Mass media	Family life and sex knowledge	

FERTILITY STATISTICS

For the United States as a whole, annual birth rates decline from a post-World War II peak in 1957 to a low point in 1968 and then rose slightly in 1969 and 1970. During the slowdown in birth rates there was a progressive downward trend in the average number of children ever born to women under 30 years of age. However, among all married or formerly married women 35 to 39 years of age—whose childbearing is essentially complete—the number of children ever born per thousand

GEORGE L. WILBER

women increased from 2,247 in 1950 to 3,225 in 1969. A similar change is found for married or formerly married women 25 to 29 years of age, where the number of children born per thousand rose from 1,654 in 1950 to 2,038 by 1969. At present it appears that women born in the early 1930s will complete their childbearing with the highest fertility since women born in the 1880s (U.S. Bureau of the Census 1971b).

In contrast, women born in the late 1940s are starting childbearing at a much slower pace than women born ten years earlier. In 1969, women under 30 had fewer children than women of comparable age in 1960. Married or formerly married women in the prime of their childbearing years, 20 to 24 years of age, show a marked increase in childlessness; in 1960, one-fourth had no child, and in 1969, one-third. It is too early to know whether this decline reflects changes in the timing of childbearing, changes in eventual completed family size, or is merely transitory.

The proportion of women in the childbearing ages has fluctuated considerably for the past 50 years. From 1940 to 1960 the total population increased about 36 percent, but the number of women in the childbearing ages increased only 13 percent. For the thirty years from 1920 to 1950, women 20 to 29 years of age (when birth rates are highest) represented about 35 percent of all those between 15 and 44. By 1960 the corresponding figure was down to 31 percent, only to rise again to 36 percent by 1969. This rise is a result of the "baby boom" in the late 1940s; with the larger cohorts of those of prime childbearing age, the age structure is favorable to higher fertility.

The annual number of marriages increased sharply during the 1960s as these "baby boom" cohorts reached young adult ages. This might suggest an increase in childbearing rates. However, the number of marriages is not a very good indicator of the number of births to expect in succeeding years, since women increasingly control the frequency and timing of their childbearing. From the late 1940s to the late 1950s, marriages decreased while births increased. Conversely, from the late 1950s the 1960s, marriages increased while births decreased.

Age at marriage is one of the factors known to influence the birth rate. At the national level, decreases in the median age at first marriage tend to be accompanied by increases in birth rates. Part of the high fertility following World War II had been attributed to the earlier age at marriage of young women in their childbearing years.

Various social and economic characteristics are related to the number of children born, and to the timing and spacing of the births. Many of these "differentials" are widely known and their relationships to fertility well established. In very general terms, the higher a woman, or couple, ranks on various status characteristics, the fewer the children born. Hence, the lower the educational attainment, the lower the occupational level, and the lower the income, the higher the number of children in a family. Further, women in rural areas or with rural backgrounds tend to have more children than their urban counterparts. Women currently in the labor force also tend to have fewer children, although it is not certain whether they are working because they have fewer children or vice versa.

The importance of educational attainment for fertility has long been emphasized. The most frequent observation is that fertility and educational attainment are inversely related; that is, the higher the educational level the fewer the children born. In one of the more intensive analyses, Duncan (1965) concluded that a sufficient condition for the control of fertility was the attainment of high levels of schooling or two generations of nonfarm residence in the history of both spouses. If this is the case, many Appalachian families face the prospect of uncontrolled fertility for some time to come simply on the basis of low educational attainment.

As noted earlier, age at marriage has come to be recognized as one of the important determinants of fertility. In general, the younger people marry, the earlier childbearing begins and the higher the number of children born by the end of the childbearing ages. Age at first marriage is apparently influenced by a number of forces—color and educational attainment among them. Whites tend to marry slightly later than nonwhites, and the higher the educational level attained the later the first marriage. Bumpass (1969) found that the negative relation between fertility and socioeconomic status diminishes with advancing age at marriage. Moreover, for both Catholics and non-Catholics, and for couples with and without farm background, the differential by wife's education is negative when the wife marries early and positive when she marries late. Bumpass speculates that age at marriage is more relevant to the adult roles of low status than of high status women. Women who marry young and do not continue their schooling beyond the secondary level enter directly into family responsibilities from their adolescent roles. Women who defer marriage increase their opportunities for acquiring the adult role not defined in the terms of family responsibilities.

The amount of time between marriage and first birth and between first and second births became shorter from the late 1940s to the early 1960s. Generally earlier ages at marriage during most of this period suggest that birth rates should rise, which they did until the late 1950s. The combination of earlier marriage and shorter durations of time between events contributed to an increase in fertility. The 18.4 months between first marriage and the birth of the first child for white women in the 1945-1949 period declined to about 14 months by the 1960-1964 period. Over the same period, the average of 32.6 months between first and second births was reduced to 25.7 months. Potentially, completed fertility might be relatively high as a consequence of these changes. However, it is not clear how family planning and changes in such matters as income and attitudes may influence the ultimate outcome. There is evidence that families with relatively low incomes have children sooner after marriage than those with higher incomes; if subsequently they should achieve higher incomes, their childbearing may leave them with relatively large families.

"And the poor get children" continues to hold true. By income or by any of the customary standards of judging poverty, birth rates are high among the poor. For all wives in poverty 14 to 39 years of age in 1967 there were 3,704 children ever born per thousand wives, which compares with 2,295 for those above the poverty line. In other words, in 1967 the typical wife below the poverty line in the United States averaged 1.5 children more than the wife not in poverty (U.S. Bureau of the Census 1971a). Comparable figures for Appalachia are not available, but wives below the poverty line in Appalachia are not likely to have fewer children than the national average for the poor.

FERTILITY IN APPALACHIA

Birth rates for Appalachia tend to follow the national pattern, but there are notable differences. In 1930 the rate of 30 births per thousand in 190 southern Appalachian counties was nearly half again as large as the national crude birth rate (DeJong 1968). By 1960 the birth rate for these counties had dropped to 23, or almost identical with the national average. The general fertility rate—the number of births per thousand women of childbearing age—showed essentially the same pattern.

Within any given population, the number, spacing, and timing of births vary around an average. Appalachian people are not essentially different in this respect from others. Although there are relatively large numbers of low income people in the region, fertility tends to vary with income, education, occupation, and by metropolitan and nonmetropolitan residence. In Appalachia, as elsewhere, we find the highest rates of fertility among those with the lowest incomes, the lowest educational levels, the lowest occupational levels, and living in rural or nonmetropolitan areas. Yet, despite a high degree of poverty and the extensive rurality of Appalachia, the overall fertility of the region approximates that of the nation.

The sharp decline in Appalachian birth rates over the past two or three decades cannot readily be explained. Superficially it appears that Appalachia is going through a demographic transition. One speculative explanation of the declining numbers of births lies with the heavy losses of young people through migration. In many Eastern Kentucky counties during the 1950s, net migration losses ranged from 50 to 70 percent of women 20 to 24 years of age (Bowles and Tarver 1965). Losses through migration of this magnitude are bound to reduce the number of children born in the area. The general fertility rate would further decline if the outmigration were among the most fertile women but this kind of information is unavailable.

Another possible explanation is that childbearing decreases if attitudes and values relevant to fertility change. There is some indication in DeJong's study that Appalachian women have come to prefer two or three children, or about the national level of preference. However, family planning programs have yet to permeate Appalachia in a very significant way, especially in the more rural areas. Educational levels and urbanization have increased, but much of Appalachia remains nonmetropolitan and average educational levels remain under the high school graduation level.

In brief, there is no adequate explanation for fertility trends and patterns in Appalachia. In addition to updating information on Appalachian fertility, there is a need to examine systematically the various potential determinants of fertility. To the extent that high fertility is related to one or more poverty properties, it is very probable that fertility control would help reduce poverty. Yet, at present, attempts to control fertility in the hopes of reducing the impact of economic poverty must proceed on the basis of scanty, incomplete, and inadequate information about fertility, its determinants, and its conse-

GEORGE L. WILBER

quences. Maternal and infant deaths are closely related to childbearing and also serve as sensitive indicators of the general health and well-being of a population. High rates of maternal and infant mortality are associated with both high fertility and economic poverty. Infants are especially susceptible to diseases which are typically reflected in relatively high death rates. In the United States a remarkable improvement in infant mortality has taken place since the beginning of this century. The infant mortality rate—the number of deaths of infants under one year of age per thousand live births—was 99.9 in 1915. By 1940 this rate had dropped to 47.0, and by 1968 to 21.7 This trend reflects improved health facilities and services. Infant mortality apparently has declined throughout Appalachia as well. The reduction in infant mortality in Kentucky, for example, followed the national trend, dropping from 74.7 in 1915 to 28.7 in 1961 (Ford 1964).

Neonatal deaths have also decreased. For the nation as a whole, neonatal mortality rates—deaths of infants under 28 days old, exclusive of fetal deaths, per live births—were only 15.8 in 1968, compared with 28.8 in 1940. The neonatal rate for Kentucky in 1959 was 19.4, or 40 percent lower than in 1940 (Ford 1964).

Fetal deaths, as expected, have followed the general decline in neonatal and infant mortality. The fetal death rate for the United States—the number of deaths (stillbirths) for which the period of gestation was 20 weeks or more per thousand live births—declined from 23.9 in 1945 to 15.6 in 1967. In Kentucky, fetal deaths dropped by about half over the two decades after 1940.

Infant deaths tend to be concentrated most heavily in the southeastern and southwestern states—areas often characterized as rural poverty areas. Consequently, despite reductions in infant mortality, areas such as Appalachia tend to suffer by comparison with more prosperous areas.

Maternal mortality, like infant mortality, has been reduced over the years. Since 1951 maternal mortality in the United States has decreased more than 90 percent. One of the chief reasons for reductions in both infant and maternal mortality is the fact that a very large majority of births now take place in hospitals, where medicines, facilities, and professional medical services are most readily available. In economically poor communities, however, the relative lack of facilities and services leads to higher mortality rates. As noted in *The People Left Behind* (1967:59), "In 1964, one-third of the 1,343 maternal deaths in the

United States were mothers in rural areas and small towns of less than 10,000 inhabitants located outside metropolitan counties."

Some Appalachian counties are without a hospital or medical doctor. In many of these same communities, fertility rates are high. The net result is that women in these communities remain under a high degree of risk of having children and dying or having their babies die.

In essence, the foregoing discussion has been concerned with determinants and consequences of fertility. Isolation of the multiple relationships between fertility and poverty is not a simple matter. Both poverty and fertility are complex variables. Poverty itself, as indicated in chapter 2, is like an umbrella that can cover many things. If poverty is conceived of only as low income, relationships between poverty and the number of children ever born fail to come into clear focus. The several properties of poverty result in a complex of poverty whose component parts may be related to childbearing in different rather than similar ways. Fertility too is a complex variable. Traditionally, natality is defined as the number of children ever born in a cumulative sense or within some specified time period, such as a year. For populations there are numerous definitions and measures of natality, and answers to questions depend in part on particular definitions and measures. Cohort and period fertility rates, for example, measure different aspects of fertility. There is now a growing interest in the timing, spacing, and planning of births as well as in the numbers born. Attention is being directed toward questions of sequences of births and other life events— graduation, marriage, employment, migration, illness, and so forth.

Despite the difficulties of conceptualizing poverty and fertility and the relationships between them, it remains reasonably clear that persons below the official poverty threshold have relatively numerous children. Women in Appalachia are among the poor who are put at a further disadvantage by large families. Children born into low income families in Appalachia—or elsewhere in the United States—suffer numerous handicaps by virtue of having "chosen the wrong parents." Hence, regardless of other important aspects of fertility and poverty, we should not delay putting into action programs and services that would help alleviate low income problems until ultimate answers are provided through research; it is important that effective services be provided to low income families to help them have only the number of children they want and can care for adequately. In the next chapter, attention is focused on family planning services.

RESEARCH NEEDS

Although enough is known about fertility trends, differentials, determinants, and consequences for program purposes, there is a need to update what is known and to probe topics where information is relatively lacking. At this writing, data from the 1970 census of population are becoming available and should be useful in examining changes in fertility for Appalachian counties, cities, metropolitan, and nonmetropolitan areas. Alterations in trends and differentials can be related to a variety of items of information available in census reports, vital statistics, and other data.

Despite what is already known about relationships between children born and education, income, employment, type of residence, age at marriage, race, and other factors, there are potentially important aspects of childbearing where information is lacking and also where general knowledge needs to be confirmed for the Appalachian area. (1) The recent decline in fertility in the United States, apparently paralleled in Appalachia, has not been adequately explained; nor at present is there a convincing basis for predicting whether the decline is purely temporary or not. The trend in childbearing as well as the reasons underlying it have obviously important implications for family planning services and facilities. (2) The timing and spacing of births in relation to the number of children born has not yet been adequately examined, either in general or in Appalachia. The dynamics of why women in low income families tend to marry early, bear their first child soon after marriage, and bear large numbers of children are not thoroughly understood. (3) The number, timing, and spacing of births need careful evaluation in relation to other properties of poverty—handicaps, unemployment, lack of education and training, frustrations, social isolation, low social mobility, and so forth. (4) The casual indications that the Appalachian region has been undergoing a demographic transition need to be confirmed or refuted. If the processes of demographic transition are in fact operating, births as well as deaths gradually come under control and the vital rates decrease. Low and balanced birth and death rates do not guarantee that low income families will have few children, but the chances of doing so should improve.

7 Family Planning Services

George L. Wilber

NATIONAL FAMILY PLANNING POLICY

Voluntary family planning has become a prevailing pattern, practiced in some fashion by almost all couples, regardless of income, class, religion, or color. Whether Americans are able to choose freely if and when to have children depends largely on the priority devoted to policies, research, and educational programs designed to reduce unwanted pregnancy.

The policy position of the United States regarding family planning is still emerging but has already undergone a considerable evolution. Since earlier days when advocates of birth control such as Margaret Sanger were jailed for their efforts, the nation has come to a position of encouraging and promoting family planning programs, both within the United States and abroad. Spokesmen for the federal government have ranged over the full continuum of possible positions on family planning. Abraham Lincoln once said that the Lord must love the common people because he makes so many of them. Dwight Eisenhower, speaking about population in 1959, said, "I cannot imagine anything more emphatically a subject that is not a proper political or governmental activity or function or responsibility." Four years later, Eisenhower retracted that statement in an article in the *Saturday Evening Post* (October 26, 1963). In it he stressed governmental responsibility for finding some realistic means of containing the population explosion. John F. Kennedy referred to the population crisis as "staggering." In his State of the Union Message in 1965, Lyndon Johnson promised to seek new ways to deal with the explosion in world population and the scarcity in world resources. Johnson repeatedly emphasized the need for freely available, voluntary family planning. In a message to Congress in 1969, Richard Nixon proposed, "We should establish as a national goal the provision of adequate family planning services within the next five years to all those who want them but cannot afford them."

A number of specific recommendations for improving and expanding family planning programs have come from such federal commissions as the National Advisory Commission on Rural Poverty (1967) and the Commission on Population Growth (1972). In essence these recommendations call for expanded public, voluntary family planning services to reduce unwanted fertility and to improve the health of pregnant women and of their children. As a means for furthering family planning, recommendations also cover areas of sex education, liberalization of abortion laws, and elimination of restrictions on access to voluntary sterilization. To the extent that these kinds of recommendations are implemented, there should be substantial progress toward the development of programs based on a national population policy which will include the principle of voluntary family planning.

The emerging policy, as reflected by presidential and other statements, is the result of numerous events and actions that cannot be detailed in this discussion. There was, for example, the 7-2 decision of the United States Supreme Court in 1965 nullifying the Connecticut anti-birth-control law on the grounds that the law was an invasion of privacy. Also in 1965, the Secretary of the Interior Stewart Udall directed that family planning be made available on a voluntary basis to Indians, Eskimos, and other groups. Between 1965 and 1968 Senator Ernest Gruening of Alaska asked witness after witness in public hearings whether they thought the federal government should help disseminate information about family planning. A large majority favored government help.

Since 1967, Congress has provided support for family planning services within the Agency for International Development and the Office of Economic Opportunity. The Family Planning Services and Population Research Act of 1970 provides for funding and encouragement of family planning throughout the nation. Primary objectives are:

1. To assist in making comprehensive, voluntary family planning services readily available to all persons desiring such services.

2. To enable public and nonprofit private entities to plan and develop comprehensive programs of family planning services.

3. To develop and make readily available information on family planning and population growth to all persons desiring such information.

4. To evaluate and improve the effectiveness of family planning services and population research.

THE NEED FOR SUBSIDIZED FAMILY PLANNING SERVICES

An important question in connection with family planning services is the extent and nature of the need for such services. Several aspects of the problems of family planning services can be identified in the following profile of women in need of subsidized family planning services in 1966 (Office of Economic Opportunity 1968). Nearly two- -thirds of these women lived in cities and over half were in the 110 largest metropolitan areas. Nearly half of the women lived within "poverty areas"—officially designated as such under the poverty program. About seven out of ten women were white and more than 85 percent lived in families which supported themselves. Nearly half of the women worked at some gainful occupation at least part of the year and about 20 percent were employed full time. Seven out of eight women had lived in the same county over the preceding 12-month period; two out of three had not moved at all. A large majority were or had been married and about 60 percent were married and currently living with their husbands; one out of six was single. On the average these women had completed eleven years of school, but about one-fourth had only a grade school education. Half of this target group was under 30 years of age and seven out of ten at the time had three children or less.

Estimates of the numbers, locations, and characteristics of women and men who require subsidized services is critical to programs for service delivery. Initial estimates can be useful as benchmarks to help evaluate the success of service delivery and to help detect changing needs for services. Unfortunately, the task of constructing estimates of this need is not easy.

The number of medically indigent women in need of subsidized family planning services was estimated at 5.3 million as of 1966. This figure was arrived at by applying the Dryfoos-Polgar-Varky (DPV) formula to estimates of women aged 18 to 44 (Office of Economic Opportunity 1968). These women are defined as fertile, exposed to the risk of an unwanted pregnancy, and medically indigent (i.e., those below the poverty and near-poverty levels as defined by the Social Security Administration). The DPV formula, developed in 1964, attempts to approximate the number of women in need by using available socioeconomic and demographic information. This formula is not designed to define eligibility, but merely to estimate the level of services needed. In calculating the number of women exposed to the risk of unwanted childbirth, the formula assumes that low income parents want three children on the average. Potential adopters of family planning either do not want as many as three children or already have had three children. The proportion of families with annual incomes below $3,000 was taken as an estimate of the poor and near-poor. The formula assumes further that about one-fourth of the women of child-bearing ages are not in need of services due to impairment of fecundity, or because they are pregnant or actively seeking a pregnancy. Finally, an adjustment is made for differences in cash income between farm and nonfarm families.

Campbell (1968 and 1969) estimated the number of poor and near-poor women in the United States in need of family planning assistance at 4.6 million as of 1966. As with most estimates, a number of assumptions were necessary. It was assumed that couples had been able to control their fertility successfully for an indefinite period of time, an assumption which overlooks the fact that many of the poor had already borne more children than they wanted. The estimate was based on a total of 8.2 million women 15 to 44 years of age in March, 1966, who were classed as poor or near-poor according to the criteria of the Social Security Administration. Three kinds of subtractions were made from this total. (1) The number of women who would not need contraception because they were pregnant with a desired pregnancy or were trying to conceive was estimated at 1.1 million. (2) An estimated 1.1 million women were subtracted because of sterility. (3) Women not exposed to sexual intercouse were estimated at 1.5 million. These assumptions are necessarily shaky because of the thinness of underlying data, and the estimate of 4.6 million in need of family planning, Campbell feels, is probably low.

New and improved estimates of the need for family planning services can be based in part on data from the 1970 census of population (Jaffe

1971). Special tabulations of the census data would indicate the number of women by age, income, family size, and marital status not only for the nation as a whole but for states, counties, cities, and other subdivisions. This data base should permit more adequate estimates of the number of women in need of family planning assistance. Census data will not show exposure to sexual activity or the number of persons who lack access to family planning services.

Of the estimated 5.4 million medically indigent women in 1968 in need of subsidized family planning services, only about 800,000, or 15 percent, were receiving assistance (Office of Economic Opportunity 1968). Of the nation's 3,000 counties, 1,200 offered family planning services by public or voluntary hospitals, health departments, or other agencies. In many of these counties, however, the number of patients served was so small that they can hardly be considered as offering aid in family planning. More than 60 percent of all counties had no identifiable family planning program of any kind; hence, an estimated 1.4 million women in need in these counties were without access to assistance. What are the effects of family planning services for those most in need of subsidized services—that is, the poor? Family planning has been argued strongly as a means to help solve the problems of economic poverty. Sheppard (1967) sums up most of the arguments in his plea for an improved and more extensive family planning service system. He maintains that:

1. Poverty is attributable in part to large family size.

2. Progress in reducing poverty in recent years is greatest among small-sized families.

3. Low income women have more children than they want because of such factors as unawareness of effective methods, insufficient income, and unavailability of family planning services.

4. The poor respond effectively to family planning services where programs have been made available.

5. The benefits of a comprehensive family planning program are significant for the reduction of poverty and of costs to the community.

The costs in dollars of unwanted children are far greater than the price for subsidized family planning services. Relatively high fertility rates among the poor obviously increase public expenditures through welfare payments, special education and training programs, and anti-poverty programs. Campbell (1968) estimated that the total economic benefits of preventing unwanted births would average $7,800 for every

GEORGE L. WILBER

$300 spent on family planning services, a ratio of benefits to costs of 26 to 1. Campbell also estimated that some eight million poor and near-poor women had 451,000 unwanted births in 1966, which represents about one-third of all births to the poor and near-poor and over 10 percent of all births in the United States. A substantial number of these births probably occurred in rural areas or to women with rural backgrounds.

The mother and her family might benefit in a number of ways by postponing or avoiding an unwanted birth. There are the obvious costs of raising a child to adulthood which might easily run upwards of $6,000. For some, unwanted births mean limited prospects for employment and reduced opportunities for their children. A woman might be able to work, or to work for a longer period of time, if an unwanted birth is prevented. Over a four-year period at an average annual income of only $3,000, the woman gains by $12,000. These figures are speculative, but they help emphasize the economic gains that might be achieved with the prevention of unwanted births.

Social and psychological costs for both individuals and society are much more difficult than the economic to identify and evaluate. For some, the costs are measured in increased family stress and unhappiness, modified life plans, and less time and attention for each child. Further, a woman has more time and energy for non-motherly activities if she avoids having a child or an additional child. Unwanted pregnancy sets off a chain of events which may drastically reduce the life chances of some young people. Unwanted childbearing also is related to such serious consequences to health as prematurity, mental retardation, infant and maternal mortality, and neglect and abuse.

ACCEPTANCE OF FAMILY PLANNING PROGRAMS

The acceptance of family planning as a personal or private issue and the acceptance of family planning programs are closely related but different things. A program is obviously more likely to succeed in meeting its objectives if it has public acceptance. Some people may accept family planning as a personal matter but reject services of a program. It is unlikely, however, that one would reject family planning for himself and then participate in a program of family planning.

There is considerable evidence that people in rural as well as urban areas are prepared to accept both family planning and family planning services. In order to achieve a goal of substantial adoption of the practice, or participation in the program, some publicity and convincing may be necessary. This raises a host of questions as to the best means of making a program effective. Various procedures and strategies have been tried and some seem to work better than others. Research has been conducted, and needs to be continued and extended, to help evaluate the merits of specific courses of action.

In very broad and general terms, Bogue (1969:826) suggests some of the essential ingredients of a successful family planning program:

1. A necessary prerequisite for an effective program is the development of an awareness of the possibility and benefits of family planning. In principle, a program should try to reduce the proportion of a population that is unaware and aware-but-neutral. Little time should be spent on the disbelievers.

2. Those who are aware of the program and react positively to it must know what to do in order to achieve the benefits. They need to know where to go, whom to see, what to ask for, what it will cost them, and how to use what they are given. Perhaps they should know about alternative methods and the reputed advantages and disadvantages of each. However, it is possible at some point that time, money, and personnel would be wasted in overinforming people.

3. The subject of fertility control should be brought into the scope of public attention as rapidly as possible without increasing the level of negative awareness. The objective is to impersonalize and desexualize the topic of family planning.

4. Legitimize family planning, primarily through private informal personal interactions. Studies show that comparatively few can be convinced of the merits of trying something new on the basis of cold, logical arguments. The endorsement of one or more respected individuals is needed. Once a person adopts a practice, he needs social reinforcement from his friends and neighbors.

5. In order to get action in family planning, knowledgable and respected people with favorable attitudes must become involved. This self-involvement leads a person to make a commitment.

6. Supplies should be available through convenient and nonpunitive channels. Some programs punish people by forcing them to wait or by making them travel long distances to get supplies. Others punish by forcing clients into embarrassment or humiliation.

There are many ways in which these principles can be applied, and

GEORGE L. WILBER

some ways are better than others. Some specific techniques and strategies may work well in one particular situation but not in another. There is a strong need for continuing and innovative research to help determine which procedures work best and under what circumstances.

One determinant of childbearing and the acceptance of family planning is the number of children desired. At the national level, most of the recent studies on American fertility find parental desires within the range of two to four children. A recent review of studies of family ideals provides useful general information (Blake 1966). The mean ideal family size for white women in the United States ranged from a low of 2.8 in 1936 to a high of 3.6 in 1961. On the average, men typically want either the same number or fewer. Preferences for two to four children have prevailed since the 1930s, suggesting that family-size ideals do not respond quickly or greatly to wars, depressions, or economic prosperity. Differences within the two-to-four-child range indicate that the two-child family has declined in popularity as the four-child family has become more "ideal." Family-size ideals increase consistently with age of white female respondents, which may be a function of changes in socioeconomic status and in attitudes toward childbearing as individuals move through the life cycle. As Blake concludes, it may be desirable to study in detail the childbearing preferences both of the older and of the reproducing generation, because of influences the older group may have on the younger.

Family-size ideals tend to vary by income, educational attainment, rural-urban residence, and other factors. Blake found that persons with a grade school education favored families one-third to one-half a child larger that persons with a high school or college education. (Since those with a high school education had family-size preferences similar to those of the college-educated, the major differential is between those with elementary education and those with more schooling.) When age, religious affiliation, and residence are controlled, the inverse relationship between education and ideal family size tends to persist.

How are reproductive goals related to actual childbearing? Blake (1967c) observes that, for white married or formerly married mothers in 1960 who have essentially completed their childbearing, actual performance falls short of the ideals, whatever the educational level. Mothers with an elementary level of education show the closest correspondence between ideal and actuality, while the greatest discrepancy occurs among the college-educated.

FAMILY PLANNING SERVICES

As might be anticipated, comparison of women with four or more years of college with those having only an elementary education shows that the latter have completed families approximately half-again as large as the former. Further, among white mothers in 1960 who had no more than eight years of schooling, distinct differences in childbearing are apparent. For white women aged 30 to 34, an average of 4.5 children had been born for those reporting no schooling as compared with 3.1 children for those with eight years of schooling. Thus, for women at the lowest educational levels, there appears on the average to be about one-half to one child over the ideal numbers. The prospects for removing this educational differential rest largely on access to the means of contraception, ability to use such means, and notions about ideal family size.

The acceptance of family planning programs in rural areas has been a matter of some disagreement. The tendency to concentrate family planning programs in areas of heavy population concentration—urban centers—can be justified on the basis of providing services to the largest numbers of people at the lowest cost per unit of service. The opinion has even been expressed, however, that it is a waste of time, personnel, and money to bring family planning to impoverished rural areas because such services would not be appreciated nor accepted. Fortunately there is a growing body of evidence which indicates, on the contrary, that low income, uneducated, rural people will accept family planning and use it effectively.

Acceptance of family planning in rural areas can be illustrated by the Alabama experiment (Bogue 1968:389-412). Six generalizations are suggested. (1) The rural poor approve of family planning overwhelmingly. Data do not support the idea of a high fertility culture. (2) The rural poor will accept family planning service of high quality when it is within their economic capacity and the limits of their ability to travel to a clinic for service. (3) A high proportion of rural couples who accept family planning methods continue their practice for sustained periods of time. (4) As a result of the first three findings, birth rates of the rural poor can be reduced more quickly than previously thought possible. (5) Special problems accompany efforts to provide family planning services in rural poverty areas; these problems are either unique or much more important than in urban areas. (6) It is practical, economical, and possible to establish family planning in rural areas.

In the clinic-plus-education program in Alabama it was concluded

GEORGE L. WILBER

that family planning services can be offered through public health clinics to families of low income and education in very backward rural areas with prompt and substantial acceptance if accompanied by an appropriate program of education for family planning (Bogue 1966). The Alabama experiment also indicated that a medical service program without an educational program tends to have less success. In the 13-county test area there was an immediate and substantial increase in the number of new patients coming to the clinics, but there was almost no increase in other rural counties of the state. Surprisingly, some of the most successful counties were the most rural, the poorest, and the least educated. In general, the success of the family planning program appeared to have little to do with the level of income, education, or degree of urbanity.

In the Eastern Kentucky Family Planning Study (Bogue 1966), women of all birth parities and ages used the family planning services. A preponderance of women in the program were relatively young and therefore had many years of potential childbearing ahead of them. At least one-third of the clinic patients learned of the program through the information campaign conducted in conjunction with the study. After the first ten and one-half months, the Eastern Kentucky family planning program appeared to be reaching women effectively. There were an estimated 25 percent who were dropouts during the first year, but the adopters were likely to experience fewer childbirths. Results of this study suggests that mobile birth control clinics or programs operated by outside organizations would have less success than clinics locally organized and operated.

Since about 1960 there have been a number of attempts to stimulate reductions in childbearing among illiterate villagers of developing nations (Bogue 1969). Results thus far are encouraging, as can be illustrated by family planning experiments in Comilla and Pho-tharam. Both programs were conducted in highly rural agricultural populations and both succeeded in getting a significant proportion of people to adopt family planning. In both cases the most illiterate and landless laborers were more inclined to accept and to persist in family planning practices than were the more educated and urban villagers.

In Comilla, East Pakistan, a pilot project for family planning was established in nine rural villages in 1960. The methods used were the conventional ones—the condom and vaginal foaming tablets—and the materials were sold to the villagers. The innovation of family planning was introduced by a person chosen by the villagers themselves from among their fellow villagers. After two years it was found that: (1) there was no apparent difference in the educational level of the adopters and the general village populations; (2) landless couples were more prone to adopt family planning than the general population; and (3) the illiterate and the landless adopted just as readily and persisted just as well as those with education and land.

In Pho-tharam, Thailand, a predominantly rural district, an action program for family planning advice and appliances was initiated in 1964. Fertility surveys inventoried the knowledge, attitudes, and practice of family planning before the action program began and at the end of the twelve months. At the first survey, two-thirds of the women had no knowledge about methods of contraception, but a year later only 12 percent were in this category. The second survey also showed that over 60 percent of the women who knew about the program had heard about it from friends and over half of the women had talked about the program with their husbands.

Family planning programs in the Appalachian region have been relatively slow in developing despite much evidence of a readiness for family planning among the people and a need to curb high fertility rates. Richardson (1969) reports that until the 1960s few patients received real family planning services in nine southeastern states—Alabama, Florida, Georgia, Mississippi, North Carolina, South Carolina, Virginia, Tennessee, and West Virginia. Although North Carolina's program in the state health department dates back to 1937, the first clinic in Tennessee did not open until 1964. West Virginia did not begin family planning services until the 1960s. Florida and Alabama serve only about 20 percent of the poor women who want and need birth control assistance. Virginia and West Virginia serve less than 5 percent. Out of the 634 counties in the nine-state area, 105 could not supply any patient data.

Richardson (1969) feels that many counties offer only vaginal foam and condoms with no medical supervision, organized patient recruitment, or evaluation. Follow-ups of patients who fail to return for appointments have been rare. County health departments have paid little attention to making access to services convenient. Critical shortages of professional and organized health resources exist in some parts of most states. In the most rural areas the prospects are dim for attracting a sufficient number of physicians to expand family planning

GEORGE L. WILBER

programs. Some communities have trained and used paraprofessionals successfully. Mobile units have been tried in Alabama with some degree of success, but in most states previous attempts to deliver health services through the use of mobile units have met with negative reactions. Despite the many problems, services in these states have grown and improved since about 1963.

RESEARCH NEEDS

The foregoing discussion helps to identify some of the research tasks in the broad area of family planning assistance. For a variety of reasons, many observers view family planning services as a means of solving one or more problems—population growth, health, economic poverty and so forth. In the emergence of population-related policies, one principle seems clear—couples should have the number of children they want, when they want them, and only that number. This implies further that services and facilities must be made available, especially for those who cannot afford them.

This kind of policy position sets the stage for family planning programs and for research and evaluation. The funding and establishment of family planning programs is accelerating. However, the need for continuing and new research in the area of family planning services is perhaps stronger now than in the past. Despite relatively abundant research on childbearing and family planning, there is much yet to be learned. The need to know more about rural people and rural areas is especially strong in view of the history of high fertility, migration to cities, severely depressed economic conditions, and the growing demand for equality of opportunity between rural and urban areas. Relatively underdeveloped regions, such as Appalachia, afford an excellent opportunity to investigate the many facets of childbearing and family planning services. Also, despite rather substantial experience during the 1960s in organizing and actually operating family planning programs—many of them abroad—there is still much to be learned about the most effective and efficient way to control childbearing.

It becomes a matter of fundamental importance to determine the reproductive goals of individuals and couples. Studies concerning the ideal and expected numbers of children must be continued and factors influencing reproductive goals need even more careful analysis than they have received up to now. For regions such as Appalachia there is a relative lack of information on such goals, largely because most studies have been national in scope. There is also little information on how changes over the life cycle affect reproductive goals. It must be ascertained how closely these goals coincide with actual childbearing, and factors that influence the attainment of reproductive goals must be identified more precisely.

The desire or demand for family planning services should be determined on a continuing basis and for small areas, as was done in the OEO study. For planning and for evaluation of existing programs, this is a critical kind of information. On the methodological side, improvements might be made in the techniques for estimating the need for family planning service. In the absence of more adequate base data, assumptions necessary to the estimates are indeed very shaky. This kind of difficulty will not be overcome quickly or easily, but its importance justifies concentrated efforts toward producing better results.

Cost-benefits studies of family planning services also require continuing research. Here, too, a number of assumptions are used, many of which are difficult to defend. Assumptions regarding the costs of raising children, for example, are based on extremely gross data. Ideally, costs of this kind should be determined for a variety of cases; for example, for rural and urban families, low income and high income families, white and black families, or for other specific categories of people, such as welfare clients in Appalachia. Cost-benefit ratios are calculated easily enough, but more than purely dollar information should be included. The fact that social and psychological costs and benefits are extremely difficult to determine does not negate their importance. Obviously, considerable work must be done before such noneconomic cost-benefit ratios can be of value.

The mutliplicity of factors determining the acceptance of family planning services constitutes still another area for research. A relatively great amount of research has already been done, the results of which have rather quickly been adopted by practicing agencies. Despite the work and progress so far, there have been relatively few studies specifically related to Appalachia or to the rural poor in the United States. It often appears that local circumstances differ sufficiently to affect the speed and completeness of acceptance. In any event there are clear indications that every family planning program should incorporate an effort to examine the factors which influence its acceptance.

Various models for the delivery of family planning services have

GEORGE L. WILBER

been proposed and tried. Standards by which delivery systems are to be judged are not entirely clear or consistent. However, the evaluation of alternative delivery systems continues to be important. From both the immediate and the long-term perspectives, information on the relative success of delivery models—organization, communication, referrals, recruitment and training of staff, retention of clients, and the like—is vital to effective family planning service delivery. Continuing and longitudinal research as well as intermittent investigations are necessary to help determine what works best under particular sets of conditions.

Studies of the effects of family on childbearing have tended to concentrate on the demographic effects, which are important in their own right, of course. Within the context of poverty, however, there is a need to assess more carefully the effects of family planning on the number, timing, and spacing of births as this in turn influences one or more of the several properties of poverty. Having fewer children as a result of family planning may improve the economic situation of a family and may protect or improve the health of the mother and, probably, other family members. But what does this mean for the motivation of the mother and father? Do they tend to aspire more strongly to higher income levels? Do they actually succeed on rising above the poverty threshold? These and other questions will remain unanswered until further research efforts are made.

In conclusion, circumstances are encouraging for a major attack on excessive fertility. The climate of opinion is favorable and family planning programs are already under way in many communities with support at national and state levels. There are strong reasons for believing that control over childbearing will reduce many of the problems of low income people. Therefore, to help assure the success of family planning services, a greater and more concentrated research effort is vital.

8   Modernism and Poverty

Thomas E. Hammock & Jon M. Shepard

One of the poverty components listed in chapter 2 is a poverty of capability, or the absence of capabilities as expressed in the underdevelopment of skills and abilities. Unemployment, underemployment, and low income levels are properties of poverty which result from poverty of capability. This chapter will focus on some psychological factors—modernism and internal-external control—that influence the extent to which persons will attempt to develop their capabilities. These two related concepts shed light on some psychological obstacles to self-support that exist among the poor.

MODERNISM

Modernism refers to a set of attitudes, values, and beliefs. As a psychological concept, modernism characterizes individuals rather than social structures. The personality characteristics associated with modernism are traits thought to aid persons in adapting to a modern or developing society.

In the conceptual development of traits of modern man, two important measurement efforts or modernism scales have evolved: the Overall Modernity (OM) scale (Smith and Inkeles 1966) and the Modernism I scale constructed by Kahl (1968). The conceptual aspect of each scale is pursued below.

Inkeles's (1966) OM scale emphasizes nine value and attitudinal themes which he feels characterize modern man but are genarally absent in traditional man. Modern man:

1. Shows a readiness and openness for new experiences. He welcomes change and innovation.

2. Possesses a facility for forming and expressing opinions on a variety of issues. The ability to form opinions concerning topics outside one's immediate enviroment is an especially discriminating characteristic of modernity. For example, Daniel Lerner (1958) in his Middle East study asked people to imagine themselves as the leaders of their country and in this role to advise how the country's problems could be resolved. Lerner found that readiness to give such opinions was directly correlated with the education of the interviewee and with the modernization level of the interviewee's country. Modernity is also characterized by a democratic approach to various opinions. The person is aware that opinions contrary to his own exist, and he is not overly defensive about such opposing opinions. Furthermore, a person with a democratic approach to opinions is not swayed unduly by the attitudes of others of high status but is equally willing to accept ideas from the young or others of lower status if these ideas have merit.

3. Is not oriented toward the past but rather to the present and future. He accepts time schedules in a positive manner, and he values punctuality and regularity in everyday affairs.

4. Attempts to plan and organize events in his life.

5. Is convinced of his own personal efficacy. He belives that he can master his enviroment rather than that he is a tool of his milieu.

6. Believes that the people and institutions in his enviroment are calculable or "dependable." Acting on calculability, modern man feels he can depend on the people and institutions around him to fulfill their allotted responsibilities.

7. Believes in the dignity of others and acts in accordance with this belief.

8. Has faith in science and technology.

9. Believes in distributive justice. Belief in distributive justice is the expectation that rewards will be contingent on contributions and not on whim or personal characteristics unrelated to contributions.

In addition to these nine themes, which cut across most types of behavior, Inkeles believes that modern man is also characterized by certain attitudes and behaviors relating to social institutions. Inkeles (1966:145) has included in his OM scale questions relevant to such institutionally related behaviors as "restriction on family size; treatment of older people and obligations to one's parents and relatives; the importance of social change; the role of women, especially the rights of women; how to bring up a child; attitudes toward religion; attitudes toward the consumption of material and physical goods; social and political problems of the community, the nation, and the international realm; educational and social aspirations, including aspirations for social mobility; and contact with media of mass communication."

In contrast, Kahl (1968:210) concluded from the development of his Modernism I scale that modernism was best characterized by seven of his subscales. These seven subscales are:

1. Activism, conceptually the same as efficacy in Inkeles's list.

2. Low stratification of life chances, which reflects the belief that one can move up in the occupational status hierarchy.

3. Low community stratification, or the conviction that one can have an effect on community policy.

4. Low integration with relatives, that is, the belief that one should not be too closely tied with the extended family.

5. Individualism, or a desire to be independent of close ties with co-workers so career goals can be pursued competitively.

6. Mass media participation.

7. Preference for urban life.

As observed, only one of these subscales—activism—parallels a personality characteristic of Inkeles's list. Kahl's other six subscales fall into the category which Inkeles calls the relationship between a person and various social institutions.

What are the processes through which men learn to be modern? Inkeles discusses the manner in which four forces—education, urban environment, mass media, and governmental institutions—effect in individuals the modern characteristics mentioned above. Two forces pertinent to this chapter—education and urban enviroment—will be discussed here as illustrative of his viewpoint. Mass media and modernization receive attention in chapter 10.

The most important force, the educational system, not only provides the content knowledge necessary to adjust in a modern society, but more broadly, it inculcates the importance of rationality and technical competence. Futhermore, the grading and evaluative systems in schools accustom students to objective standards and to the principle of distributive justice.

THOMAS E. HAMMOCK and JON M. SHEPARD

An urban environment exposes one to new experiences and to rapid change and forces him to adapt to innovations. Also, the absence of those sanctions that bolstered traditional patterns in the village facilitates change in the new urbanite. Furthermore, Inkeles (1966:14) notes that by "exposing men to a variety of ways of living, a wide range of opinions and ideas, increased mobility, and more complex resources . . . [the city] accelerates the process of change" and, in addition, " in many cities, there are powerful examples of rationality, of the use of technology to master the physical demands of life, of rewards adjusted to technical skill and competence, of the value of education, and of the guarantee of human dignity under law."

MODERNISM AND INTERNAL-EXTERNAL CONTROL

Several scholars have called for a clarification of the status of the concept of modernism in relation to other psychological concepts. Although there is no research specifically on this point, one psychological variable seems to be intuitively connected to some facets of modernism. Rotter's concept of internal-external control (1966) seems particularly related to Inkeles's self-efficacy and Kahl's activism subscales, both of which refer to the tendency to believe that one can cope with and influence one's environment. Since Inkeles and Kahl found that the activism and self-efficacy factors were most central to their larger scales, the internal-external control variable appears to be related to the most significant variable of each.

Rotter proposes a personality dimension (the I-E dimension) that concerns the degree to which a person believes the rewards and punishments he receives are produced by his behavior. Those who feel that the reinforcements they receive are determined by fate or chance rather than by their own actions are termed extensively controlled (E-Cs); those who believe their rewards and punishments are functions of their own behavior are classified as internally controlled (I-Cs). Because E-Cs believe forces independent of their actions determine their well-being, they tend not to learn or perform behaviors that would better their circumstances. Rotter summarizes the research on I-Cs (1966:25), pointing out the contrasts with E-Cs. "A series of studies provides strong support for the hypotheses that the individual who has a strong belief that he can control his own destiny is likely to (a) be more alert to those aspects of the enviroment which provide useful information for his future behavior; (b) take steps to improve his environmental condition; (c) place greater value on skill or achievement reinforcements and be generally more concerned with his ability, particularly his failures; and (d) be resistive to subtle attempts to influence him." It is easy to see that the I-E variable is either closely related to or synonymous with the activism and self-efficacy factors.

A counseling technique for changing external to internal orientations is being developed by Reimanis (1970). In this technique a counselor meets with highly external persons either in small groups or individually twice a week for ten weeks. In these sessions, while subjects (all E-Cs) talking about themselves and their problems, the counselor uses the following methods. First, he negatively reinforces external statements such as "I'm in college because my father wants me to be," and "I'm in college because I feel I ought to be an M.D." Second, when a subject mentions a problem, the counselor asks him to think of various alternatives he had for avoiding the problem and of ways he could avoid similar problems in the future. Third, the counselor encourages the subject to make decisions that are based on what he himself desires. Because self-efficacy and activism are similar to the I-E variable, this method should at least increase a participant's level of activism and self-efficacy and perhaps his level on other aspects of modernity. Lower socioeconomic groups especially could profit from this technique because they are generally more external than are higher status groups, as Battle and Rotter show (1963).

THE RELEVANCE OF MODERNISM AND INTERNAL-EXTERNAL CONTROL FOR CAPABILITY POVERTY

How are modernism and internal-external control relevant to capability poverty? One of the central dimensions of modernism—activism (Kahl) or self-efficacy (Inkeles) and internal-external control pertains to a person's belief in his own capabilities. It seems reasonable to conclude that the more a person believes in his ability to master his environment and is inclined to exert effort in that direction, the greater will be his capabilities. A person who feels that he can help himself through job training is more likely to gain the knowledge and skill which will actually promote self-support.

The psychological factors discussed in this chapter have been applied

THOMAS E. HAMMOCK and JON M. SHEPARD

in the poverty-related areas of fertility and family planning on the one hand and job training on the other. Fertility and family planning are less directly related to capability poverty than is job training. Still a relationship exists between the extent of childbearing and capability poverty and self-support. It is in poor families that the woman's income is most needed. Yet high fertility may work against either employment or the acquisition of skills requisite for employment because it ties the woman closer to home. Therefore, the reduction of fertility may decrease capability poverty because females would presumably be freer either to pursue activities which promote the development of abilities and specific skills or to take and maintain employment.

Research in the area of fertility and family planning has been conducted with the OM and Modernism I scales. One possible application of the OM scale might be in predicting those most likely to adopt birth control methods. A study by Williamson (1970) is relevant to such an application. Specifically, Williamson attempted to predict from two independent variables whether a person favored birth control—the person's ideal family size and his feelings of self-efficacy (that is, feelings that he can cope with, and have an impact on, his environment). The items for measuring the three variables were all from the OM scale; three items measured favorability toward birth control, fourteen measured personal efficacy, and one measured ideal family size. Williamson's sample consisted of approximately 2,500 male factory workers, ages 18 through 32, from Chile, India, Pakistan, Israel, and Nigeria.

Williamson compared the two psychological variables (ideal family size and personal efficacy) with eleven social variables (such as education, mass media exposure, income, skill level, marital status, number of children, and age) with respect to how well they predicted favorability toward birth control. When Williamson (1970:333) calculated for all five countries the percent of variance in the favorability toward a birth control index explained by (1) the two psychological variables, and (2) by the social indicators, he arrived at the following statistics: the two psychological predictors alone predicted 11 percent of the variance in Nigeria, 1 percent in Chile, 4 percent in Pakistan, 14 percent in India, and 4 percent in Israel; the 11 social predictors alone accounted for 4 percent of the variance in Nigeria, 3 percent in Chile, 5 percent in Pakistan, 3 percent in India, and 6 percent in Israel. Although the amount of variance accounted for by the psychological variables is not large in an absolute sense, the predictive power of the psychological variables compares favorably with the social predictors provided by the Williamson data.

Kahl (1967) applied the Modernism I scale in a study of variables related to family size in Brazil and Mexico. Kahl also used the respondent's ideal family size rather than actual fertility rates, since all his subjects were young enough to have more children. He notes that socioeconomic status (SES) and metropolitan residence are negatively associated with ideal family size in Mexico and Brazil, with SES more strongly negative in Mexico and urban residence more strongly negative in Brazil.

More specifically, Kahl asked if any subscales in Modernism I account for a noticeable amount of variance in ideal family size in addition to the variance accounted for by SES and residence. The total score on the Modernism I scale was negatively associated with ideal family size, but Kahl wished to select a subscale theoretically associated with ideal family size. Although the subscales, "modernism in nuclear family roles," and "low religiosity," had both correlated negatively and significantly with ideal family size, they had been used only in Mexico. The subscale Kahl selected to predict ideal family size was "low integration with relatives"—that is, the belief that one should not be too closely tied with the extended family. The amount of variance in ideal family size explained by each of the three independent variables, SES, residence, and low integration with family (considering each variable alone) is as follows: low integration with relatives accounted for 8 percent of the variance in Brazil and 15 percent in Mexico, SES accounted for 4 percent of the variance in Brazil and 11 percent for Mexico, and metropolitan location accounted for 25 percent of the variance in Brazil and 7 percent in Mexico (Kahl 1967:106). Although these figures leave much of the variance unaccounted for, they are large enough to make meaningful predictions.

Finally, several variables related to activism were found by Keller, et al. (1970) to differentiate between black married couples who use contraceptives (users) and those who do not (nonusers). It was found that users in comparison to nonusers were higher in self-efficacy, in need for autonomy versus dependency, in need for achievement, and in tendency to plan ahead.

Research using the I-E scale shows similar results. Hypothesizing that I-C females, as compared with their E-C counterparts, would be more

THOMAS E. HAMMOCK and JON M. SHEPARD

likely to believe they could control events and thus more likely to attempt to avoid unwanted pregnancies, MacDonald (1970) gave female college students Rotter's I-E scale and asked whether they did or did not use birth control measures. As hypothesized, among those who reported premarital coitus, 62 percent (24 out of 29) of the I-Cs indicated they practiced birth control while only 37 percent (16 out of 43) of the E-Cs reported such practice.

From this research, then, it appears that people high in certain aspects of modernism would tend to want smaller families and would be amenable to practicing birth control. One might apply this information in a family planning center. If the center were limited in capacity, it might work most effectively by concentrating on those high in modernism; or, if capacity were no problem, extra encouragement might be given to participants with lower levels of modernity.

The I-E scale has additional implications beyond family planning. Consider job training. There is evidence that many of those who are likely to participate in job training programs have a lower level of internal control than other segments of the population. Specifically, it has been shown that members of lower socioeconomic classes tend to be lower in level of internal control than middle and upper classes, and that blacks tend to be lower on this scale than whites (Lefcourt 1966; MacDonald 1970, 1971; Forward and Williams 1970).

Some additional research indicates that people with an internal locus of control might do better in job training programs. For example, Rotter and Mulry (1965) found that people who are high on internal control tend to place greater value on skills and ability. Others have found that adolescent job trainees who were high in internal locus of control performed better when engaged in job training, when looking for jobs, and when on the job. It may be that efforts toward increasing internal control would promote higher performance during the job training program as well as after the completion of training.

Thus far modernism has been treated as a relatively stable trait. But what about the possibility of changing the modernity level of individuals for their benefit? We have seen that, through a counseling technique, people with an external psychological set can develop an internal orientation. Since this internal-external dimension is roughly equivalent to the activism and self-efficacy components of modernity, it seems plausible that at least this important aspect of modernism could be changed relatively easily. If modernism is manipulable in this manner, then traditional people such as those in Appalachia might be taught to be modern. For example, such a technique for developing psychological modernity would facilitate the adjustment of Appalachian residents migrating to urban settings.

However, an important caveat must be kept in mind if techniques for inculcating modernity are to be developed and applied: Psychological modernity should be taught only to those who are experiencing or who might experience social and economic modernization. A modern orientation in a traditional society would frustrate the modern person and hinder his adaptation to the traditional society surrounding him.

RESEARCH NEEDS

The foregoing discussion of the relevance of modernism and internal-external control for capability poverty is suggestive rather than definitive. Since these psychological factors have not been prominent in the study of poverty, most of the suggestions outlined above are plausible ones in need of actual research.

Is it true that the more confidence people have in their ability to control their life events, the more they will develop their capabilities? Will the inclination and capability for self-support be heightened by increases in self-efficacy, activism, and internal control? In what ways does high fertility promote capability poverty? Will modernism and internal control reduce fertility, and will reduced fertility, in turn, reduce capability poverty? There is some evidence that these psychological factors work favorable effects on fertility behavior and family planning. The connections between fertility attitudes and behavior and capability poverty are not so well documented.

Conventional research (in such forms as surveys and case studies) is always necessary and probably should be conducted first. Research and demonstration projects, however, would seem to be especially appropriate because of the interest in increasing self-support and decreasing poverty of capability. Use of techniques for increasing the level of internal control seems to be particularly promising in this regard. Attention could also be directed to creating methods for increasing self-efficacy and activism. Family planning clinics and job training programs would be excellent sites for the institution of such research and demonstration programs.

9 Achievement Motivation and Poverty

Martha Woods

It is evident from chapter 8 that several variables can be used in studying the psychology of poverty. This theme is continued in the present chapter which focuses on achievement motivation or the need for achievement. Achievement motivation was selected because it is closely related both to modernism and to economic development.

Barriers to the development and satisfaction of achievement motivation represents obstacles to the attainment of independence and self-support above a level of economic poverty. The need for achievement appears to be one of the most immediate and significant aspects of one's motivational resources. Therefore, the extent to which a person effectively mobilizes this drive is a major consideration in explaining behavior. Moreover, blockages to the satisfaction of the need for achievement may result in a special variety of poverty; that is, the motivational poverty discussed in chapter 2. In the present chapter several aspects of achievement motivation will be examined: its meaning and behavorial correlates, its relationship to economic development, its relevance to poverty in Appalachia, and, finally, its practical implications.

The concept of achievement motivation or need for achievement was formulated originally by Henry A. Murray (1938) and has been variously defined as "a relatively stable disposition to strive for achievement of success" (Atkinson 1966:12), "a generalized concern with meeting standards of excellence" (Brown 1965: 430), and a two-component motive to avoid failure and to approach success (Atkinson and Litwin 1966:76).

According to Byrne (1966:336-38), academic performance (defined on the basis of college grades, scholastic aptitude, IQ, number of years of education, and the like) is one of the most widely investigated correlates of need for achievement, and had generally been found to relate positively to achievement motivation. High need for achievement has also been found to correlate with prestige of the occupation aspired to, ability to delay gratification, failure to yield to the incorrect majority in conformity experiments; memory for interrupted tasks under achievement-oriented conditions rather than relaxed conditions, entrepreneurial skills, and sales and marketing expertise. Of special interest in this chapter is the correlation between achievement motivation and economic development.

THE ACHIEVEMENT MOTIVE AND
ECONOMIC DEVELOPMENT

Max Weber in *The Protestant Ethic and the Spirit of Capitalism* (1904) theorized that the Protestant Reformation was causally related to the development of modern industrial capitalism. Weber based his theory on historical evidence. The rise of Protestantism in Germany, Switzerland, England, and the Netherlands coincided with the rapid economic growth associated with the rise of capitalistic enterprise; Protestant entrepreneurs were more successful in the business world than Catholic entrepreneurs even though the Catholic families more often had the initial advantage of wealth. This theory, linking two large-scale social movements, attracted the attention of a psychologist of the present day, David C. McClelland, who in an attempt to make the theory more specific and testable postulated a mediating social-psychological mechanism (1961). McClelland placed the acquisition of the achievement motive within the context of child rearing practices.

In order to test his modification of Weber's thesis—that the Protestant ethic, manifested in child rearing practices, engenders a need for achievement which contributes to rapid economic development—McClelland (1961) had to explore the relationships between each pair of variables in the hypothesized sequence (see figure, p. 123).

122   MARTHA WOODS

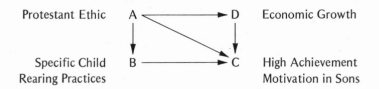

Protestant Ethic   A → D   Economic Growth

Specific Child   B → C   High Achievement
Rearing Practices   Motivation in Sons

Research bearing on each of these links follows.

Protestant ethic-economic development (A→D). By comparing all the countries of the temperate zones on levels of economic development in 1950 (measured by per capita consumption of electricity, correcting for differences in natural resources), McClelland (1961) discovered that there was a significant difference in the level of economic development favoring the Protestant countries. This piece of evidence is considered supportive of Weber's portion of the theory.

Protestantism-child rearing practices (A→B), and Protestantism-achievement motivation (A→C). Using a representative sample of the population in the United States, Veroff et al. (1960) administered to parents a questionnaire on independence training and then measured the achievement motivation of their sons. The findings indicated the Protestants set slightly earlier ages for independence than did Catholics; however, the difference was not statistically significant. A comparison of achievement scores also yielded an insignificant difference; furthermore, the slight difference favored the Catholics.

In support of the relationship between Protestantism and need for achievement, McClelland (1961) reports that, in a comparison study of two nearly equivalent villages in Mexico, one of which was Protestant and the other Catholic, assessment of the achievement motivation of schoolboys by the graphic method (Aronson 1958) demonstrated that boys of the Protestant village were higher in need for achievement than the Catholic boys. However, Brown (1965:464) interjects a word of caution about McClelland's finding: "There were numerous difficulties about comparing the data in addition to the doubt we must have about the validity of the graphic measure."

These results call into question the notion that Protestantism necessarily leads to early independence training and high achievement motivation. It must be concluded, in light of this evidence, that simple nominal affiliation with a religious denomination is not a crucial variable in the chain of events, at least in the modern world. Brown (1965) suggests that holding constant the influences of socioeconomic level, ethnicity, and religious fervor is a necessary precaution in such comparative studies. McClelland (1961) concluded that the relevant variable is generally a value or group of values that could be represented in any religious group, rather than church affiliation per se.

Child rearing practices-achievement motivation (B→C). Investigators have hypothesized that the need to achieve is acquired through child rearing practices which stress the importance of competition, excellence of performance, and independence. Most, although not all, of the research is generally supportive of the hypothesis and can be summarized by citing a few representative studies. Cox (1962) found a significant relationship between achievement motivation and the number of household duties and responsibilities in which the child said he participated. Winterbottom's research (1958) showed that mothers of boys with high need to achieve expected independence demands to be met at an earlier age than did mothers of low achievers; that differences between the mothers were not a result of number of demands made but rather of the kinds of behaviors demanded; and that more mothers of high achievers responded with physical affection (kissing or hugging) when their sons were learning to meet these independence demands than did mothers of low achievers. Rosen (1959) reported that when parents are asked to give estimates of how well their sons will do on a certain task, parents of high-need achievers give higher estimates than parents of low achiever boys.

It can be concluded with some certainty on the basis of these empirical findings that the development of achievement motivation is influenced by the way children are reared. Since there are social class differences in child rearing practices (e.g., in independence and achievement training), further support for the association between achievement motivation and child rearing practices is indirectly given by the finding that middle class adolescents are higher in need for achievement than are lower class adolescents (Rosen 1956).

Achievement motivation-economic growth (C→D). In examining the relationship between the achievement motive (measured by content analysis of various forms of representative literary writings) and national rate of economic growth (measured by, for example, electricity consumed per capita), McClelland (1961) consistently found that increases in the rate of economic growth could be predicted from prior levels of achievement motivation. This finding was substantiated for the

MARTHA WOODS

United States during the years 1920 through the 1950s, for Spain for the fourteenth through the sixteenth centuries, and for England from the beginning of the fifteenth century through the beginning of the Industrial Revolution in 1830. Similarly, the thesis has been tested for other countries and other time periods and, as predicted, the results have generally indicated that high levels of achievement motivation are present in advance of economic development.

Having considered the evidence, it seems that the strongest links in the thesis are the relationship between need for achievement and economic growth and the relationship between child rearing practices and need for achievement. Further, these two links are interrelated; and, in fact, McClelland's most recent formulation makes this connection. On the basis of solid evidence, McClelland states that a particular value orientation leads parents to practice early independence training with their children. This produces adults who may be labeled entrepreneurial characters (Brown 1965). The resulting entrepreneurial characters, who have high achievement motivation as one of their traits, can then be recruited to entrepreneurial roles and be in a position to promote economic growth.

THE RELEVANCE OF ACHIEVEMENT MOTIVATION TO POVERTY IN APPALACHIA

Achievement motivation is an important variable in the study of poverty in view of its direct relationship with economic development; but the evidence which shows that achievement motivation is low among Appalachian people is indirect, since no studies have been done which compare the achievement need of the Appalachian people with that of the people of this country in general. The supporting evidence which can be adduced comes from data which describe such characteristics of the Appalachian people as education, occupation, and income levels. Indices of these variables indicate that the Appalachian region has a smaller percentage of the population over 25 years of age at high school and college educational levels, a smaller percentage in the higher prestige or entrepreneurial positions, a smaller per capita income, and higher rates of unemployment than the United States population at large (see, for example, U.S. Census of the Population 1960; Hansen 1970; Losman 1970; and Widner 1970). Since educational level, occupational prestige, and income correlate positively with achievement motivation, it is possible to make the tentative inference that low levels of achievement motivation are characteristic of the Appalachian people in general. Although this inference must be considered tenuous until it is tested by actual research, it is worthwhile to attempt to identify factors in the Appalachian region which foster low achievement motivation. Two such factors, relative lack of achievement-oriented role models and the absentee control of natural resources, are considered here.

Heckhausen (1968) suggests that imitation learning from models (e.g., parents and other adults) appears to be an important factor in the acquisition of motives. Presumably this process is important also in determining the means by which the motive is satisfied. Thus, if it is true that Appalachian people are generally low in achievement motivation (at least in economic and occupational areas), it may be that the lack of entrepreneurial characters in the area leaves no effective models with whom the maturing children can identify. The lack of real models to observe or to interact with on a day-to-day basis may even vitiate potential effects of achievement-oriented models that Appalachian youth come in contact with through the mass media. Child rearing practices of the region may also be implicated as a cause of low occupational achievement motivation.

Another variable which may be related to the presumed low level of achievement motivation is the natural resources situation in the region. There is no dearth of natural resources in Appalachia; it is rich with coal and timber land and is secondarily noted for various metals, nonmetals, crude petroleum, and natural gas. However, the crucial element of the natural resources complex is the manner in which these resources are managed. It is well-documented that these resources are controlled, for the most part by absentee owners and that most of the wealth derived from the resources is pumped out of the area; in general, the people of the area neither control the riches nor benefit from them in such a way as to enable them to break out of poverty (see, for example, Burlage 1970; Barkan and Lloyd 1970). The implication of absentee control of the resources is that achievement motivation is unlikely to be maintained in a system which provides negligible opportunity and reward for personal achievement and initiative; thus, in Appalachia the incentive to achieve in economic areas is minimized.

There is the possibility that the level of achievement motivation can be raised. The development of high levels of achievement motivation

MARTHA WOODS

would conceivably reduce motivational poverty and increase self-support. There are several points at which intervention might bring about higher levels of achievement motivation. One such point is child rearing practices; there are, however, some problems with intervention here. Child rearing practices are quite difficult to change. Futhermore, the evidence supporting the relationship between child rearing practices and levels of achievement motivation is simply not strong enough to justify drastic social action. A greater quantity of research of a more comprehensive nature is required before such action could be considered on a large scale.

The next possible intervention point is the academic setting. For example, by training underachieving high school boys (those whose grades were low as compared to their IQ scores) to know the characteristics of the person with high achievement motivation, Kolb (1965) was able to improve their school grades. This improvement was evident for students of high social class but not for those of low social class in a follow-up study 1.5 years after the training. McClelland (Harris 1971) mentions that in Syracuse, New York, the public schools in a black community have developed a test program for instilling the need for achievement by training. It might be worthwhile to establish similar programs in the Appalachian schools for all age groups.

It might also be possible to train adults to be high in achievement motivation as McClelland and Winter (1969) report they have done in India, Mexico, Spain, and the United States. In a distributed brochure, the training program used was described as a course for developing motivation for management. Participants were businessmen, approximately 30 to 45 years of age, who responded to the brochure. Training included experience with behaviors which are associated with high need for achievement, such as moderate risk taking and goal setting, in order to familiarize the participants with the achievement syndrome. Training techniques consisted of case studies, role playing, "educational games," and small group exercises. Participants were prodded to relate the achievement syndrome to their own careers, goals, and values, and to set goals for themselves in terms of the course outcome. The course was conducted in an interpersonally warm, supportive group atmosphere since research indicates that motivational changes are more likely to occur and to be maintained under these circumstances.

Follow-up studies based on a number of psychological and business-activity variables were conducted two years after completion of the training program. The results indicated that, for several of the training groups (e.g., Bombay businessmen and executives in a large United States corporation), there was significant increase in their business activities following the course. McClelland and Winter (1969:357) argue that the results can be understood as follows: "It appears as if the instruction in achievement was one of the important means by which the men became convinced that they themselves were entirely capable of expanding their business activities." McClelland and Winter (1969:350-56) list and describe other successful programs conducted in a variety of settings.

It is possible that the system of absentee control of natural resources could stand in the way of developing similar programs designed to raise the level of achievement motivation in Appalachia since, as we have seen, absentee control tends to minimize reward for initiative in economic activity. A possible solution is to replace the absentee system with local ownership or, at least, local management. Support for this intervention is inherent in McClelland's theory of achievement motivation which states that economic growth will not take place unless those of high achievement motivation (assuming the presence of high achievers) are recruited to entrepreneurial or managerial positions. The absentee system prevents this; those who presently control the resources recruit Appalachian men primarily for worker positions in a continuation of an earlier categorization of the mountain people as cheap labor (Barkan and Lloyd 1970). It seems a justifiable conclusion that any program designed to improve the economic situation of the Appalachian people must attempt simultaneously to raise the level of achievement motivation of the people and to effect changes in the management of natural resources. As a consequence, those with high motivation may find satisfaction for this need in local economic activity. Further, the wealth derived therefrom may be kept in the region to act as capital for stimulating further economic expansion. McClelland and Winter's findings (1969) offer strong support for such changes in the opportunity structure. It must be kept in mind, however, that to stimulate the motive to achieve and/or to raise levels of aspiration without simultaneously increasing accessibility to the means of achievement could create frustration and high levels of alienation.

In chapter 2 it was recommended that primary attention be given to poverty properties that could be changed. Largely because of the psychoanalytic viewpoint that personality development virtually stops at the age of six, most psychologists have felt, until recently, that the levels of such traits as achievement motivation and the activism component of modernism could not be appreciably changed in adolescents or adults. From the evidence cited here, it appears that achievement motivation can be considered a poverty property that is alterable. Indeed, many social scientists believe that at least some personality traits can be changed much more easily than was formerly thought, as McClelland and Winter (1969:377) note: "Man is not as predetermined in what he can do as social scientists and historians sometimes think. He has greater freedom to act, to change the structure of his response, and find opportunities in the environment than the traditional forms of social analysis would lead him to believe."

RESEARCH NEEDS

It seems evident, then, that much research is needed for clarification of the variables which control the development and maintenance of achievement motivation. One important area of future inquiry is the existing level of achievement motivation among the poor. Do the poor actually have less achievement motivation or do they, for lack of real or perceived opportunities, merely appear to have a low level of achievement motivation?

Another area of research is the link between child rearing practices and achievement motivation. Are they related? If so, are there techniques for changing child rearing practices?

Experimental programs which would implement McClelland's procedure for improving motivational levels and subsequent entrepreneurial activity would be another promising area of investigation, because the procedure satisfies the important criteria of applicability and effectiveness. That such a training program might be feasible in the traditional Appalachian culture is indicated by the experience of McClelland and Winter's training sample in India (1969). The traditionalistic small businessmen in this sample were able to profit from the training in spite of encountering problems similar to those facing Appalachian men (e.g., they had trouble getting licenses from the government for scarce raw materials, were forced to spend what money they could save on supporting their extended families rather than on business investments, and so on). Overcoming these obstacles, the traditionalistic participants were just as likely as the modern men to become active in business-related matters following the training. Furthermore, the feasibility of a similar program in Appalachia—at least on a small scale—is demonstrated by the fact that a project to increase the motivation for power has recently been carried out in Appalachian areas of Kentucky for 104 residents of the area who work for various community agencies (cited in Harris's interview with McClelland 1971). The program has apparently been successful.

In addition, in a research proposal submitted to the Office of Economic Opportunity by the Behavorial Science Center of Sterling Institute (1969), it is stated:

With slightly different objectives, depending upon the area of achievement in which the group is involved, this kind of training has been conducted and evaluated by BSC/SI in India, Uganda, Australia, Canada, and among scores of groups in communities throughout the United States. Groups who have been trained in this country have included businessmen in depressed urban and rural areas, under-achieving high school students, salesmen, business managers, executives, CAP directors, CEP directors and staff, and community action workers and staff, and CEP course participants from the Mexican-American community. Research has shown that, in such groups regardless of cultural setting or work environment, between 60% and 70% of the course participants significantly changed their behavior after training.

Some other areas of research worth exploring include the relationships between achievement motivation and fertility and migration. The relevance of research on fertility among the Appalachian poor can best be illustrated by noting the high birth rates which, although on the decline, are characteristic of these people (see, for example, Belcher 1962). Obviously, high fertility rates create even greater tension in the already strained economic situation. Do parents with high-need achievement have fewer children than low-need achievers? Understanding the fertility-achievement motivation complex would lead to more effective family planning projects and would demonstrate the value of altering the level of achievement motivation.

Are high-need achievers more likely to outmigrate than low-need achievers? Do they adapt to the environment to which they migrate better than low-need achievers? Is there any change in the level of motivation following migration? The usefulness of exploring the achievement motivation-migration relationship depends primarily on the long-range goals of Appalachian planning; that is, whether programs to benefit the impoverished will be aimed at encouraging them to leave the area or at encouraging them to remain with the hope of economic development within the region. If the latter goal is sought, to find that high-need achievers are likely to outmigrate would make it sensible to set up economic incentive programs which make it worthwhile for them to stay in the region. To avoid interfering with the present economic and occupational systems in the region is to allow outmigration to continue to be a feasible alternative to Appalachian subsistence. And if it is those high in need achievement who tend to outmigrate, this is but another natural resource lost to the region, another mechanism helping to perpetuate the impoverishment of the people who remain.

10 Communication and Modernization in Appalachia

Daniel E. Jaco & Philip C. Palmgreen

The physical and sociocultural isolation of Appalachia has maintained
the existence of nineteenth-century ideas and technology within the
boundaries of the most affluent nation in the world. While there are
subcultural elements within Appalachia which may be preferred to their
modern counterparts, the consequences of this isolation for the people
of the region—whether one considers general health, income, education,
or almost any of a number of other variables—have for the most part
been highly disadvantageous. Therefore, the infusion of modern norms,
ideas, and innovations, carefully articulated with present Appalachian
culture, is required if the gap which continues to increase between
urban America and rural Appalachia is to be diminished.

Modernization may be viewed as a process by which individuals (and
/or societies) change from a traditional way of life to one which is more
complex, technologically advanced, and undergoing rapid change
(Rogers 1969:14). It is no longer sufficient to conceive of this process
strictly in economic terms; nor is it sufficient to echo the simplified
solution of the technical specialist who sees development merely as a
diffusion of scientific knowledge to areas where such knowledge previously existed either in slight measure or not at all. Rather, we should
view modernization and development from the perspective of the social
scientist who "looks upon technological development as change in

patterns of the culture and society" (Foster 1962:9). Modernization, then, involves concomitant changes in the entire cultural fabric of the target system. It will be useful, as an initial step, to examine the target system—the traditional subculture of Appalachia.

THE SUBCULTURE OF TRADITION

Rogers (1969:25) cites ten elements he feels to be central to a traditional subculture. Donohew and Singh (1969) found most of these elements represented in the characteristics of poor Appalachian farmers. The ramifications for the successful diffusion and adoption of innovations in Appalachia should become evident as the chapter progresses. Although isolated conceptually for examination, the elements should be conceived of as functionally interdependent.

1. *Mutual distrust in interpersonal relations.* The element of mutual distrust in the mountaineer's relationship with others is supported by Weller (1966:163), who notes a leveling tendency in the culture, lack of status seeking, disinclination to join groups, and ability to function in a group only on a personal basis. Cain (1968) highlights the role of suspicion in the interpersonal relations among Appalachian residents.

2. *Perceived limited good.* Foster (1965:293-315) contends that tradition-oriented people commonly hold to the notion that all desirables in life (e.g., land, wealth, health) exist in finite quantity, are always short in supply, and cannot be increased in supply. It follows, therefore, that one can improve his own position only at the expense of others. Although this variable has not been investigated in an Appalachian context, it is easy to see why such a characteristic might be found among the poor inhabitants of this region.

3. *Dependency on and hostility toward government authorities.* In Appalachia, a long history of exploitation at the hands of outsiders has in large part conditioned the rural residents to a hostile view, as convincingly documented by Caudill (1962), Weller (1966), and Barkan and Lloyd (1970). Weller speaks in terms of "independence-turned-individualism" in the mountaineer's way of life, a corruption of the old virtue of independence. When he accepts a welfare check and returns to the hollow to pursue his own ends, he portrays his dependence quite clearly.

4. *Familism.* The subordination of individual goals to those of the family, typical of the mainstream of nineteenth-century America, is

evident in Appalachia today, although it seems to be slowly diminishing.

5. *Lack of Innovativeness.* An innovation is defined as an idea, practice, or object perceived as new by the individual (Rogers 1969). Appalachian residents are tradition-oriented and slow to innovate. It is likely that this is a function of life pattern, generations of negative cultural conditioning, and lack of capital.

6. *Fatalism.* Fatalism is the degree to which an individual recognizes a lack of ability to control his future. Weller (1966:37-40) proposes it as a principal element in Appalachian culture.

7. *Limited aspirations.* A sense of fatalism, the image of limited good, and the reality of blocked opportunities have undoubtedly conditioned Appalachian residents to low aspirations. One of the main components of this element, achievement motivation, is dealt with in detail in chapter 9.

8. *Lack of deferred gratification.* The failure to postpone immediate satisfaction in anticipation of future rewards may be averted only by those with more-than-adequare resources, a rare condition among Appalachian residents.

9. *Limited view of the world.* Time perspective and general orientation (whether internal or external to one's social system) are two cultural components of a limited view of the world. The mountaineer is primarily oriented to the past and present while the modern urban dweller has developed future-time orientation. Particularly intimate is the relationship between lack of future-time orientation and a prevailing sense of fatalism. The mountaineer is also localite—that is, oriented within his own system (Weller 1966:30)—as compared to being externally oriented (cosmopolite). Two variables that are likely to be of considerable importance in reducing localiteness are geographical, or physical, mobility and exposure to mass media.

10. *Low empathy.* The ability of the Appalachian resident to project himself into the role of another person is obviously restricted by his limited contact with individuals in different roles. As such, low empathy acts as a "mental insulator" against cosmopolite influences such as the mass media.

Identification of these ten elements widens the range of potential research. Comparatively few systematic studies have been conducted which deal specifically with communication and modernization in Appalachia. However, a rather large literature concerned with communication, change, and modernization has grown out of research in developing countries wherein the culture of the bulk of the population has been noted to exhibit these general elements. In fact, Redfield (1956:25) and Foster (1962:45) have both argued for the universality of a peasant or traditional subculture. If the main elements of any traditional subculture can be identified, then much of the groundwork for making cross-cultural generalizations and achieving a meaningful synthesis has essentially been laid. At worst, such an approach is of heuristic value and with potentially far-reaching implications.

Appalachia, however, does not constitute a "monolithically homogeneous mountain culture" (Bowman and Plunkett 1969:102) as may have been implied above. Schwarzweller and Brown (1969) define it as a rural society in transition; Lewis (1970:6) flatly states that "Appalachians are bicultural"—that most Appalachians learn and belong to mainstream culture and their mountain subculture at the same time. Lewis (1970:14) further asserts, "Programs for change must recognize the varieties of Appalachian life styles and avoid uniform programs to eliminate poverty based on distorted stereotyped pictures of Appalachian life."

What are the implications of these tradition-oriented life styles for social programs? The relationship between communication, modernization, and social services should be obvious. Unless individuals have knowledge of and, further, have internalized modern norms, values, and practices with regard to such matters as nutrition and family planning, there is little reason to expect a high degree of social service utilization and participation in these areas. Even where a particular service is being substantially utilized, there is no guarantee that it is being used in the manner most beneficial to the client. For instance, participation in the food stamp program does not insure a person an adequate diet unless he is aware of and has internalized good nutritional practices. In addition, the success of many social services depends upon the spread and acceptance of innovations such as new birth control devices. Indeed, an entire new program itself may be viewed conceptually as the innovation. Communication thus becomes a vital factor in disseminating knowledge about these innovations and persuading individuals to accept them.

The spread and acceptance of modern norms and practices would become even more crucial in the event an income (as opposed to service) welfare strategy is implemented, since it will be left up to the welfare recipient to decide what goods and services he will purchase.

Experience with public assistance has shown some of the dangers inherent in such an approach. As Weller (1966:31) has stated about Appalachia, when welfare arrived in the the 1930s "a man could accept a check and go on living up the hollows as he had always done." In other words, thus far the government has provided the means necessary for pursuing prevailing traditional goals without attempting to modernize the normative structure of the rural community (Schwarzweller and Brown 1969). How can such modernization be accomplished?

This chapter will derive its focus from one major assumption: *modernization is essentially a communication process* (Rogers 1969: 43). It is largely through communication with an external, urbanized society that modernization of normative structures takes place. Change from a traditional to a more modern culture necessarily involves the communication and acceptance of new ideas (innovations). Since traditional cultures constitute relatively closed systems, such change tends to be initiated by sources external to the social system. Communication thus becomes a vital factor in accomplishing change, and, as such, is central to modernization. Furthermore, communication is not only the essential link through which externally oriented ideas enter a traditional society, it is also an indispensable force for facilitating further dissemination within the system. One of the major sources of external ideas as well as a means for their diffusion is the mass media.

Basically, communication channels may be considered dichotomously as either mass media or interpersonal although one should not overlook the crucial role which their successful interaction plays in the modernization process. Before delving into each separately in some detail, a brief look at the differences should be helpful. Mass media communications, as compared to interpersonal communications, are distinguished by: (1) the larger potential size of audience that can be reached simultaneously; (2) a mechanical or electronic mode of transmission interposed between source and receiver (this element largely accounts for the failure of the mass media in many instances to effect attitude change); and (3) absence of mutual source-receiver surveillance (Rogers 1969:99).

THE ROLE OF THE MASS MEDIA IN MODERNIZATION

Certain aspects of the role of the mass media in the modernization process may be rather obvious, although their importance is often overlooked. For example, the mass media are great information multipliers. Interpersonal channels alone are inadequate for reaching the bulk of traditional peoples. The cost and effort to train sufficient numbers of local development workers (change agents) to reach the inhabitants of every hollow in Appalachia would be enormous. Even if such agents could be provided in sufficient numbers, many of them would have difficulty in passing the "credibility test" in an area distrustful of government officials.

Since they have been located principally in large cities, the mass media of underdeveloped areas have generally exhibited a strong urban orientation and provided a basically unidirectional urban-to-rural flow of information. This constant infusion over time of modern norms to a rural people surely produces alterations in the structure of a given community at various junctures. However, the infusion is undoubtedly impeded by the low relevancy of the messages transmitted from the urban setting and may be further weakened by the operation of such processes as selective exposure, selective perception, and selective retention (Klapper 1960).

A note of caution must be sounded here with respect to Appalachia. The majority of the mass media in Appalachia do not have strong urban orientation to the extent characteristic of the media of the underdeveloped nations. Few Appalachian residents subscribe to a metropolitan newspaper, and most listen to local radio stations only. Among the media available to Appalachian residents, only television (which *is* transmitted principally from large cities) seems to be uniformly urban in character. This is not to say that communication principles which have emerged from research in the underdeveloped countries are not valid in Appalachia, but it suggests that, in Appalachia, television may carry a disproportionate share of the modernization burden.

Research has revealed certain general principles concerning differential levels of media exposure in developing areas: (1) radio reaches the largest audiences in developing areas; (2) the electronic mass media generally reach larger audiences than the print media; (3) of the print mass media, newspapers reach larger audiences than magazines; and, (4) there is a "centripetal effect" (Lerner 1963:341), that is, exposure to one medium is positively related to exposure to other media. This positive relationship implies both desirable and undesirable consequences: multiple media exposure probably increases media influences where mass media are mutually reinforcing; however, it implies that those individuals unreached by one medium tend not to be reached by others.

In the United States, with its highly developed mass media, the adequacy of the structures and channels for communicating modernizing information is usually taken for granted. This assumption tends to overlook regional fluctuations in mass media distribution and utilization. It may be demonstrated that Appalachia, in addition to being geographically separated from the rest of American society, also suffers from an informational isolation. Moreover, there are data to support the assumption that inequalities in the distribution of information in a society may be related to inequalities in the distribution of other ingredients of social life (McNelly and Molina 1972).

Table 10.1 illustrates the differences in mass media availability levels in 1966 among Appalachian, non-Appalachian, and urban counties in Kentucky. According to these data, only about 69 percent of the households in the Appalachian counties had TV sets, as compared to about 88 percent and 92 percent for the non-Appalachian and urban counties respectively. An even greater disparity existed with regard to newspaper circulation, with total daily circulation standing at an average of 1.13 papers per household in the urban counties, .90 in the non-Appalachian counties, and .50 in the Appalachian area of the state. The differences become further magnified when one considers the circulation figures for metropolitan daily papers (i.e., those published in cities with populations of 50,000 or more, generally the most modern in content): the per household figures are 1.13 and .69 for the urban and non-Appalachian counties respectively, as against only .23 for the Appalachian counties. This might be attributed to an "accident of geography," since most Appalachian residents do not live in metropolitan areas, and thus metropolitan papers are not readily available. Yet whatever the causal chain, the differences in availability of modern urban information are real enough, with Appalachia once again exhibiting a large relative deficit of information.

The only medium which showed no readily apparent difference was radio; about 87 percent of Appalachian households reported having at least one radio. These figures are supported by Stephens (1970:17) who maintained, "Radio is a constant companion to the Appalachian poor." In a project during the period 1965-1968 for which data were collected in Knox County, Kentucky, Stephens found that all respondents in his sample (N=204) reported listening to the radio. Although no supporting

DANIEL E. JACO and PHILIP C. PALMGREEN

TABLE 10.1   Mass Media Availability Levels in Kentucky Counties

Medium	Appalachian counties (N=49)		Non-Appalachian counties (N=71)		Urban counties[a] (Fayette, Jefferson, Kenton)	
	Total	Per household	Total	Per household	Total	Per household
Met. daily circ.	53,486	.23	442,307	.69	309,434	1.13
Non-met. daily circ.	62,344	.27	137,041	.21	205	.00
Total daily circ.	115,830	.50	579,348	.90	309,639	1.13
Weekly circ.	111,322	.48	207,622	.32	37,517	.14
	Total	% of Total	Total	% of Total	Total	% of Total
Households with radios	200,940	87.1	582,630	90.4	252,480	92.5
Households with TV sets	159,900	69.3	564,010	87.6	250,900	91.9

Source: Data in Lewis Donohew and Robert K. Thorp, "Mass Media Availability Patterns in Kentucky Counties." Communications Research Monograph, School of Communications, University of Kentucky, No. 1, Summer 1966.
[a] Counties containing a city with a population of 50,000 or more

data are available, this apparently high level of radio usage may be partly attributable to the introduction of the low-cost transistor radio.

Unfortunately, the figures quoted on Appalachian radio usage are rather misleading. The majority of Appalachian residents listen only to local radio stations (partly because radio reception is severely hampered by the mountainous terrain) whose program content is generally restricted to country music. Stephens found that only one-third of the respondents in his study attended to news or public affairs items. This is significant from the standpoint of modernization. Donohew (1967:685) found in a content study of the mass media in Appalachia that there are differences in the modernizing effects of different types of media content, with news and public affairs programs at the "most modernizing" end of the continuum. He found that persons exposed to news programs make higher scores on variables indicating receptiveness to change and lower scores on "isolation" variables than those exposed only to other content types. In addition, he found that those exposed to "other content types," but not news and public affairs, made higher scores than those not exposed to the media at all. Although these findings must be qualified somewhat by noting that more modern persons may simply tend to listen to more news and public affairs programs, the causal chain nevertheless probably works both ways. It is clear that the majority of Appalachian radio listeners pay scant attention to that information which is potentially the most modernizing.

The preceding figures on mass media exposure relate to the Appalachian people as a whole. The figures become even less encouraging when we consider only low income families. For example, Johnson et al. (1967:76-78) found in a study of families participating in the program for Aid to Families with Dependent and Unemployed Parents in seven Eastern Kentucky counties:

Over four-fifths of the families had no member who reads a newspaper regularly, half of the families seldom or never saw television, and a third had no radio. Most of the few newspapers read were local county weeklies—the radio stations they reported listening to were almost exclusively local Eastern Kentucky ones. While one might expect each family to be reached by at least one of the media, this was not the case, for a fifth had no newspaper, radio, T.V., nor anyone in the family who regularly viewed T.V.

In keeping with the theme expressed in chapter 2, poverty may be measured in many dimensions; it thus appears that in addition to the well-documented poverty of Appalachia with respect to such indices as

DANIEL E. JACO and PHILIP C. PALMGREEN

income, health, and resources, there also exists a severe "poverty of information" in the region. Although the mass media were identified in chapter 2 as a regional resource, and the poverty of information as a regional characteristic, the consequences of information-poverty can be as devastating for individuals as for entire regions. And, this poverty of information may well be a major factor contributing to an individual's state of poverty along the other dimensions.

The situation in Appalachia is highly analogous in this respect to the situation in the developing countries; there, low levels of exposure to media, coupled with the inability to utilize available media, have been recognized as a crucial factor severely handicapping efforts to bring these poverty-stricken tradition-oriented inhabitants into the mainstream of the twentieth century.

An excellent organizing and explanatory device which can be used in the study of the mass media in relation to other variables is the model. The adequacy of a model lies in its ability to be consistent with empirical findings that bear on the relationships suggested by the model. One model which has been quite fruitful in testing hypotheses related to communication and modernization is shown in Figure 10.1. This model, the evolution of which may be traced through Lerner (1958), Deutschmann (1963), Rogers (1969), and Stephens (1970), assumes an implicit time element with mass media exposure as the intervening variable between antecedent variables (those which may act to determine whether an individual will be in the mass media audience or not) and consequent variables (or desired ends in the modernization process in this case). A central role is given to the mass media Roger's data firmly support this central position of the mass media inasmuch as he found strong positive relationships between each of the variables and mass media exposure. However, it should be noted that the model fails to account for the degree to which media exposure itself may contribute to antecedent variables such as enhancement of literacy, education, social status (by creating new "gatekeepers" and opinion leaders), and cosmopoliteness (an important variable to be considered in greater detail in a later section). Likewise, some of the consequent variables at times function as antecedents. Viewed with this limitation, the model clearly reveals the fact that we can be much more certain of the relevance of the mass media than of their actual effects. It does provide insight, however, into the predominant time order of these variables.

Two of the consequent variables in the model—empathy and inno-

FIGURE 10.1 Paradigm of the Role of Mass Media Exposure in Modernization

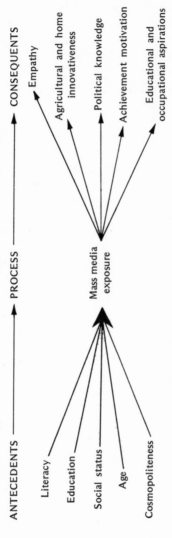

ANTECEDENTS ──────▶ PROCESS ──────▶ CONSEQUENTS

Literacy

Education

Social status

Age

Cosmopoliteness

Mass media
exposure

Empathy

Agricultural and home
innovativeness

Political knowledge

Achievement motivation

Educational and
occupational aspirations

Source: Everett M. Rogers in association with Lynne Svenning, *Modernization among Peasants: The Impact of Communication* (Holt, Rinehart, and Winston, Inc., 1969). Redrawn and reprinted by permission of the publisher.

vativeness—have received special emphasis in the literature and deserve such emphasis here. Empathy, as was noted earlier, is a kind of "psychic mobility" that allows one to imagine himself in a variety of roles. Lerner (1958, 1967), in his discussions of communication, considers empathy to be central to the process of modernization; it enables one to function within a wider environment and allows for modern messages to become more relevant. A highly empathic traditional man is more likely to be affected by exposure to mass media. Low empathy, on the other hand, mentally insulates one from modern ideas, thus rendering media inputs less effective. Of course, exposure to the mass media increases the individual's empathic skill. In fact, media exposure has been found to be more highly related to empathy than to functional literacy. Donohew (1967) using data collected in Eastern Kentucky, isolated two factors which relate to empathy: (1) a factor indicating exposure to stimuli for change from outside the community along with attitudes and behaviors indicating an orientation toward change; and (2) a factor indicating exposure to others within the community.

Innovativeness is the degree to which an individual adopts new ideas or innovations relatively earlier than others in his social system (Rogers 1969:294). It should be evident why Rogers considers innovativeness to be the best single indicator of the degree of modernization. The ultimate test of modernity for any individual is the degree to which he has actually accepted modern technological ideas, products, and practices. Innovativeness provides us with such a behavorial, as opposed to attitudinal, measure of modernization.

Measures of innovativeness have arisen chiefly from that extensive research tradition concerned with the diffusion and adoption of innovations. Rogers and Stanfield (1966) indicate that more than 1,100 published findings dealing with diffusion of innovations exist, half of which have appeared since 1960. (An extensive bibliography of research on the diffusion, or communication, of innovations is available in Rogers and Shoemaker [1971].) Diffusion is basically a communication process, in that it is the spread of awareness about an innovation, over time, via specific channels of communication, through a social system. But diffusion need not imply adoption or acceptance. Acceptance instead has come to be linked with the process of *adoption*, which, while certainly complementary to diffusion, is a distinct process conceptually and readily subject to separate analysis.

Adoption is a psychological process involving the decision of an individual or group to accept or reject a given innovation. An adoption model consisting of five stages has been found to be adequate for purposes of empirical investigation (Rogers 1962): (1) *awareness stage,* in which the individual first becomes exposed to the innovation; (2) *interest stage,* the individual actively seeks more information; (3) *evaluation stage* (sometimes called the "persuasion stage," with somewhat less justification), the individual mentally applies the innovation to his present and anticipated future situation, and decides whether or not to try it; (4) *trial,* the individual tests the innovation on a small scale; (5) *decision,* the decision is made to adopt or reject the innovation.

Time is an essential variable in the measurement of innovativeness. Most current measures simply employ the relative time of adoption (for different individuals) of an innovation or combination of innovations to form a continuous measure of innovativeness. This measure is often used as the basis for classifying persons into adopter categories. Research has shown that the time of adoption for various members of a social system generally takes the shape of a normal curve (see Figure 10.2). Adopters are classified on the basis of the mean and standard deviation of this curve.

The first category, the Innovators, include the first 2.5 percent to adopt the innovation. Innovators are eager to try new ideas, are more cosmopolite, and are venturesome. The next 13.5 percent, the Early Adopters, display greater integration into the social system than do Innovators and are more localite. This group also has the greatest number of opinion leaders. The 34 percent in next place, the Early Majority, are generally highly social, but rarely hold positions of opinion leadership. The next 34 percent, or Late Majority, tend to approach innovations cautiously, and only adopt in many cases due to economic necessity or social pressure. The final 16 percent, the Laggards, are highly localite, possess little opinion leadership, and are usually frankly suspicious of innovations. They also tend to be socially isolated, although isolation is not always the express property of the Laggards. In many traditional societies, it is the Innovators who are the outcast and who possess little opinion leadership.The implication for Appalachia is that one may expect very little impetus for modernization to originate within Appalachia itself, since the mountaineer who dares to innovate is perceived as deviant.

Curiously enough, there is a dearth of research on the characteristics of innovation rejectors. It is easy to forget that the adopter curve does

DANIEL E. JACO and PHILIP C. PALMGREEN

FIGURE 10.2 Adopter Categorization on the Basis of Innovativeness

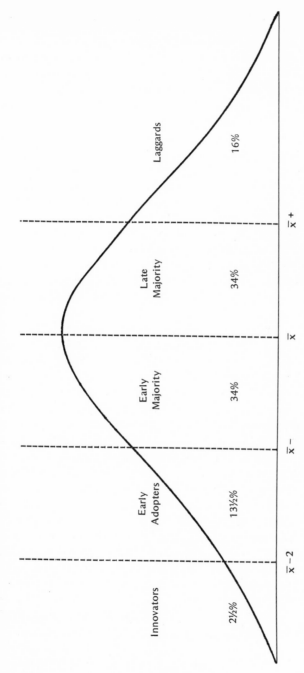

Innovators
2½%

Early
Adopters
13½%

Early
Majority
34%

Late
Majority
34%

Laggards
16%

$\bar{x} - 2$ $\bar{x} -$ $\bar{x}$ $\bar{x} +$

Source: Everett M. Rogers in association with Lynne Svenning, *Modernization among Peasants: The Impact of Communication* (Holt, Rinehart, and Winston, Inc., 1969). Redrawn and reprinted by permission of the publisher.

FIGURE 10.3 Paradigm of Modernization Antecedents & Innovativeness

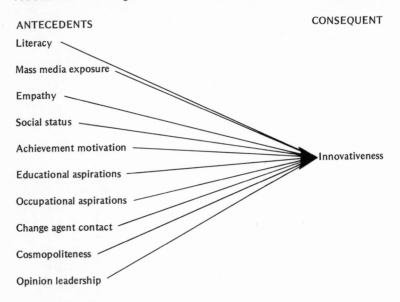

Source: Everett M. Rogers in association with Lynne Svenning, *Modernization among Peasants: The Impact of Communication* (Holt, Rinehart, and Winston, Inc., 1969). Redrawn and reprinted by permission of the publisher.

not include all members of the population, and in many cases may comprise only a small percentage. In a traditional society, therefore, those who reject the innovation may be even more backward than the Laggards, since the Laggards at least finally decide to adopt. Research into the characteristics of Rejectors might be highly fruitful in an area such as Appalachia.

The principal antecedents of innovativeness identified by past research and their hypothesized roles are shown in Figure 10.3. This paradigm, however, is oversimplified, since it ignores the antecedent role of mass media exposure with respect to such variables as empathy, achievement motivation, and educational and occupational aspirations. Perhaps a more accurate representation would be achieved by combining the essential elements of the above model with those of Figure 10.1, which describes the role of the mass media in modernization. The resulting paradigm is shown in Figure 10.4.

DANIEL E. JACO and PHILIP C. PALMGREEN

FIGURE 10.4 Model of the Role of the Mass Media in Innovativeness

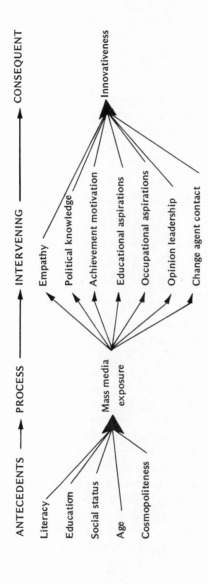

Source: Everett M. Rogers in association with Lynne Svenning, *Modernization among Peasants: The Impact of Communication* (Holt, Rinehart, and Winston, Inc., 1969). Redrawn and reprinted by permission of the publisher.

This model once again emphasizes the role of the mass media in modernization. However, it also underscores the indirect relationship between exposure to mass media and the decision to innovate. This is not to say that the mass media cannot effectively transmit technical details about an innovation; it is simply that the relationship between mass media exposure and innovativeness may result from the creation of a favorable mental set toward change (as shown by the model) rather than from the transmission of specific details about innovations. In creating such a "climate for modernization," the mass media have an important role in furthering innovativeness—a role which in media-poor areas such as Appalachia may not be realized to its full potential.

One may thus infer that, if large flows of information in the service of rapid social change are not successful, they are at worst only ineffective. Yet, concern must be manifested for the negative ramifications of massive, modern inputs into a traditional system. Caudill (1968) indicates that while empathy levels rose among youths in Knox County, Kentucky, alienation levels also rose. This suggests that rising expectations may be countered by the frustration which occurs when expectations are insufficiently paralleled by opportunity and availability. Lerner (1963:333) has referred to this phenomenon in terms of the "Want:Get Ratio."

Furthermore, the creation of new elites in a society that is undergoing rapid transformation might well have a detrimental impact on the social structure, with the resultant disequilibrium constituting a threat to the stability of the system. One way in which systems can cope with this problem is by the selective channeling of advice-seeking to the individuals in the society already relatively high in the economic and affiliative hierarchies. Chu (1968) found that those of high status in a traditional culture will often strive to maintain their status by using the media to update themselves on relevant information. This is an instrumental function which media can serve. On the other hand, media users of lower economic and affiliative ranks are seldom consulted by others; this absence of social reward reduces the motivation to make use of media information. Thus, if the system dispenses social reward to some and withholds it from others, the disequilibrium "caused " by the introduction of mass communication in a traditional social system can be reduced. How applicable this remedy is for Appalachia is open to question, since mountaineers have been noted to exhibit a leveling tendency and lack of status seeking. However, to reiterate, Appalachia is an area experiencing transition. An interesting question grows out of a concern for the instrumental function of media: which content portions of the media are perceived as instrumental by the target population and for what reasons? Instrumental communication has usually been defined, or assumed, by the researcher on the basis of his own value system or internally consistent rationalization. The need for future research to gather data on the perception of instrumentality has been identified by Whiting and Stanfield (1972), and its value is unquestionable for an area where too many assumptions may already have been made in the past.

Discussions of mass media inputs as modernizing elements often give the impression that one need only transmit a sufficient number of such inputs to set in motion a "climate" for change. This may in a large sense be true; yet at the same time it is misleading. What is missing is the recognition of the importance of interpersonal communication in the modernization process.

THE ROLE OF INTERPERSONAL COMMUNICATION

Early development in communication research reflected models of society and images of man then current in other social science disciplines (Halloran 1970:9). Sociologists at that time conceived of society as a "mass," or a vast aggregate of isolated individuals lacking unifying purpose. The current psychological notion of man was as a nonrational species with a relatively uniform basic human nature. The apparent effectiveness of World War II propaganda, in conjunction with these concepts, imputed to the mass media an omnipotence they never deserved. Although there are some who continue to subscribe to such a notion under given specified conditions, the "hypodermic needle" model, whereby mass media inputs are simply injected, as it were, into a population to produce widescale attitude change, was largely invalidated when Katz and Lazarsfeld (1955) demonstrated the "role played by the people" in the mass communication process. Bauer (1964) refers to "the obstinate audience" in explicit rejection of the mass as a monolithic, passive recipient of mass communication messages.

The significance of interpersonal communication can easily be seen in Ithiel de Sola Pool's (1966:101-2) poignant explication of the interaction between "new" and "old" channels of communication in a modern society:

Modern means of communication seldom replace the previously existing means. Television has not eliminated radio; radio has not destroyed the printed book; the invention of print has not stopped us from writing letters by pen and ink; and teaching people to be literate does not make them any less inclined to converse. Each new mode of communication is superimposed upon the old. It may take over certain functions, but other functions are retained by the former mode.

Thus, in the communication system of the most highly developed societies, there is a complex interaction between the modern mass media system and the traditional network of personal word-of-mouth communication. A modern society is not an anomic depersonalized mass society free from primary groups. It is an elaborate system of families, clubs, ethnic groups, classes, political organizations, and friendship groupings.

The dissemination of any idea or practice in such a society depends not only on the publicity it is given in the mass media but also in conversation and discussion about it among people, face-to-face. The mass media provide people with basic information; but before people will act on such new information, they need to be encouraged by people in their immediate environment whom they know and respect. Farmers may learn about a new agricultural practice from hearing a broadcast. They are likely to adopt it only when they see a neighbor getting a better yield by using this practice.

Pool's statements generally are valid with respect to a modern, highly developed society. Studies in the United States confirm the primary role of the mass media at the awareness stage of the adoption process, but emphasize the preeminence of interpersonal channels at the evaluation, trial, and decision stages (Lionberger 1960, Rogers 1962). However, in Rogers's (1969) Colombian study, none of the peasant respondents made any mention of mass media channels at any stage of the innovation decision process. Although the media presumably had an indirect effect through change agents, interpersonal channels (especially fellow farmers) were of primary importance. This suggests that a diffusion paradigm based on studies conducted in the United States may not be directly applicable in underdeveloped countries which have low mass media availability. The similarity of Appalachia to the underdeveloped countries, especially with respect to media usage, leads to the hypothesis that a similar lack of fit with the general paradigm may be observed in this region. Because of low levels of mass media availability, Appalachian residents might be expected to utilize interpersonal channels in their adoption of innovations to a greater extent than persons in other areas of the United States.

Individuals serving as sources of information may be divided into two types—cosmopolite and localite. Cosmopoliteness, as was noted

DANIEL E. JACO and PHILIP C. PALMGREEN

earlier, is the degree to which an individual is oriented outside his immediate social system. A localite is therefore an individual whose interests are confined to his immediate social and physical environment with little or no interest in the world "outside." Among the factors which account for differences between the two types of individuals are degree of contact with other cosmopolite individuals, trips to other villages or large cities, and contact with the mass media.

It is also helpful to consider channels of communication as being either localite or cosmopolite. Localite channels originate within the social system of the receiver; cosmopolite channels have their origins outside the immediate social system of the receiver. In other words, since channel and source may not share the same orientation, a four-way distinction is to be made here—cosmopolite sources, cosmopolite channels, localite sources, and localite channels. For instance, a change agent is a cosmopolite source, but he utilizes localite interpersonal channels of communication. Theoretically, at least, a radio station existing largely as a cosmopolite channel might utilize sources (indigenous broadcasters) which could have either a buffering or catalytic effect on the audience depending upon the function performed by the source; i.e., whether the broadcasts reinforced the status quo or attempted to tailor modern messages to local conditions.

It has been found that interpersonal cosmopolite channels are more important in creating technicaltechnical knowledge about an innovation than in forming favorable attitudes toward a new idea (Rogers 1969:132). Of course, cosmopolite channels are more important at each stage of the adoption process for earlier adopters than for later adopters. Interpersonal localite channels, however, are generally more important than interpersonal cosmopolite channels at each stage in the innovation decision process.

Focusing on the individual, it makes intuitive sense that those better integrated into their social system will experience a greater amount of positive face-to-face contact with the members of the system. In more practical terms, this means that the localites, who are generally reinforcers of the status quo in a traditional culture, will be much more likely to affect the opinions, judgments, and behavior of others in that system. As long as culture remains strongly traditional in its normative patterns, cosmopolites exist as "marginals," ostracized or rejected by the society at large. Moreover, a cosmopolite in a traditional culture may undergo a substantial amount of psychological stress, since he is probably the object of strong social pressure demanding a realignment of his attitudes and/or behavior. Failure to conform to these demands may mean complete rejection by the society members. Hence, the cosmopolite role as a channel of modernizing information generally is somewhat muted in a traditional society.

In analogous fashion, one may usefully extend the discussion of the cosmopolite individual in traditional society to the cosmopolite mass media channels carrying modern messages into an unreceptive system. The low relevancy of such messages and their lack of fit with existing patterns tend to lower their modernizing impact (although they act more effectively upon any cosmopolites present in the system).

There is reason to believe, however, that the cosmopolite individual plays a more important modernizing role on Appalachia than the foregoing might suggest. Schwarzweller and Brown (1969:1) assert, "Contemporary Appalachia is predominately a rural society in transition." Cosmopolite individuals, it has been found, are less "deviant" in such a transitional society than are their counterparts in a traditional society. In a transitional society, cosmopolites are more prominent both as change facilitators and as by-products of change acceleration. Modernization creates new elites in a system. No longer do we find the pattern in which a few individuals are recognized throughout the culture as experts on a variety of topics (polymorphism). The increasingly complex flow of information, along with concomitant structural and normative changes in the system, demands the creation of information specialists who act as sources of advice and opinion on particular topics of importance to others in the system (monomorphism). The cosmopolite individual is well suited to fill this role. Also of importance is the change agent, who acts as a link between the two cultures.

A change agent may be thought of as a professional who is employed by a client to interfere actively and purposely with a target culture or subculture in the service of directed change within that culture. He (or she) is exogenous to the target system (in location and/or in orientation) and, in the case of Appalachia, functions as a systemic link (see Loomis 1959) between modern American society and traditional (or transitional) Appalachia. In essence, the change agent is a special kind of communicator interested in inducing communication events which will produce deviations from those attitudinal and behavioral patterns which impede modernization, and at the same time will encourage the adoption of new attitudes and practices (see Lippitt et al. 1958). The change agent may be either a permanent fixture of the target culture (as in the case of the agricultural extension agent) or a temporary link (e.g., the applied social scientist), in which case the agent's ultimate aim is to be sufficiently effective that he eventually serves little function in the target system.

In order to devise suitable communication strategies, the change agent needs at least a fairly extensive, if not intensive, understanding of the culture with which he is dealing. In his study of an Appalachian mountain neighborhood in Kentucky, Cain (1968:4) concludes, "No matter how beneficial an innovation is for the recipient society, chances for acceptance will increase only in proportion to the amount of energy the change agent expends in adapting his methods to the culture of the potential acceptor. Such adjustment requires an understanding of that culture." Unless the change agent takes this approach, cultural, social, and psychological obstacles will continue to constitute barriers to effective communication, as Foster (1962) points out in his classic work on barriers to change in traditional cultures.

One of the first requirements for any change agent is that he master reasonably well the language of the culture in which he hopes to be effective. It may be expected that in the Appalachian context much more verbal overlap exists between the languages of change agent and residents than would be the case in a foreign village. Yet, while this problem may not be as great for the Appalachian change agent, minimizing the disparity seems unwarranted. Cain (1968:68) observed in the Appalachian neighborhood which he studied that the vocabulary of the neighborhood was quite different from that of the "outside world." He found that words common to the two vocabularies can have entirely different meanings; in addition, he observed words absent in the vocabulary of the potential change agent which were present in the Appalachian vocabulary.

Once the change agent has mastered the language of the target culture, he has little more than a formal structure for communicating with the client population; language of itself cannot be regarded as a sufficient tool for success. Most cultural phenomena are underlain by a host of implicit thought and behavioral patterns which are reflected in the unconscious performance of its members. These nonverbal elements, such as gestural and intonational configurations, the conception and treatment of time and space (Hall 1959, 1966), comprise a communication system in many ways more powerful than the verbal. Weller (1966:67) provides an excellent description of how the nonverbal system functions in Appalachia: "Young people are not taught to listen to what words mean, but only to what emotion the speaker is conveying. Hence, it is extremely difficult for teachers, social workers, ministers, and others to communicate with mountain people." To say that the members of a culture seem to take these patterns for granted (and many apparently do so) may fail to emphasize that violation of them is readily perceivable to members and may arouse suspicion concerning the change agent.

Cain notes that the mountain dweller is aware of the "hillbilly" stereotype held by the outside world. Hence, the change agent must discard all erroneous preconceptions and demonstrate an appreciation of mountain life if he is to be accepted. Conversely, the change agent—by definition—must favor change (Deutschmann et al. 1968:39).

While the mass media can and do, of course, also act as change agents (Lionberger 1960:42-51), they lack many advantages of interpersonal channels. As a major cosmopolite influence, the interpersonal change agent is effective for several reasons. (1) Schramm (1964) has demonstrated that the mass media are primarily an urban phenomenon; he asserts that their impact lessens as one moves away from the city. The change agent, in filling the role of "middleman" or "cultural bridge," may be able to accelerate the adoption of innovations by localizing and situationally legitimizing them; e.g., showing how they apply to the Appalachian situation. Local mass media can also play the middleman role by fitting external information to local conditions and needs. (2) As a heavy user of the mass media himself, the change agent may also act as "gatekeeper," that is, filter media outputs. In this way, he can keep up-to-date on modern developments, passing along those of benefit to the target in such a way that the information is perceived by the target to be relevant. (3) The change agent is also an "interstitial person" (Bowman and Plunkett 1969:100-104), as a member of a "third culture" (Useem et al. 1963), who is located by the nature of his training, work and/or interests between two cultural systems, participating to some degree in each. As such, he functions as a feedback link between client and target that provides for more efficient decision making vis-à-vis the target. This points up the importance of viewing communication a two-way process; the change agent not only relays information to the target but exchanges information with him as well.

DANIEL E. JACO and PHILIP C. PALMGREEN

(4) As a systemic linkage between cultures, the change agent constitutes an organized and routinized communication channel by which plans are put into action. (5) Fuchs (1967:274) suggests that the "unusual" behavior of a change agent (as perceived by the target) relative to an innovation may often be accepted because he is an outsider. Indigenous innovators are often seen as deviant in a traditional social system. In such a situation, it is probably safer for those members of a culture who possess a high level of change-readiness to associate with a disruptive change agent than with a disruptive member of the same system.

To be maximally effective the change agent desires immediate personal contact with members of the target system. The personal nature of a change agent's communication activities is emphasized in Table 10.2. Moreover, in order to effect the best allocation of his very limited resources (primarily time), the change agent must necessarily be selective in choosing the individuals on whom he will focus his activities. Essentially, he wishes to create new "middlemen" and thereby increase the spread and rate of diffusion. Most change agents, therefore, tend to have greater contact with target members who are characterized by relatively greater innovativeness, higher social status, and more education. Conversely, members with change agent contact are typified by a higher degree of all characteristics of modernization, especially innovativeness. Nonetheless, a danger exists in selecting individuals who are *too* innovative. The reader will recall that "Innovators" (under the diffusion scheme), while cosmopolite, were venturesome and not generally well integrated into their sociocultural system. More likely to persuade others in the target system is the group designated as "Early Adopters," which ordinarily has the highest percentage of opinion leaders.

The change agent himself has need of certain characteristics if he is to succeed. Much has been said about the development of empathy among traditional peoples, but no studies have focused on the empathic ability of the change agent which is undoubtedly an important factor in his success. A high degree of empathy in the change agent may be found to be of critical significance by helping to compensate for the diminished effectiveness of communication when agent and client share few attributes.

Credibility, the degree to which a communication source or channel is perceived as trustworthy and competent by the receiver, is another highly important but little researched factor in change agent success.

TABLE 10.2   Use of Communication Channels by Latin American Change Agents

Channel	Mean[a]
Individual discussion	2.13
Informal individual conversation	2.11
Group discussion	2.02
Informal group conversation	1.83
Written report	1.65
Individual demonstration	1.39
Group demonstration	1.31
Memorandum	1.05
Letter	.87
Telephone	.82
Charts, graphs, or photographs for presentation to individuals	.78
Charts, graphs, or photographs for group presentation	.76
Articles in periodicals	.64
Circulars or pamphlets	.64
Movies or slides	.57
Radio or television programs	.26

Source: Paul J. Deutschmann, et al., *Communication and Social Change in Latin America: Introducing New Technology* (New York: Frederick A. Praeger, Publishers, 1968), p. 97. Reprinted by permission of the publisher.

This table is offered here as a possible useful guideline for the change agent rather than as a statement of the proper emphasis due the various channels.

[a]Based on scores from 0 (never) to 3 (much)

The more credible the source is perceived to be, the greater his persuasiveness. Future investigations should seek those factors which lead to higher change agent credibility. One general factor that has been noted to be significant in the success of the change agent is his total personality (Foster 1969:116).

Furthermore, communication between change agent and target is more effective when there exists a high degree of homophily, that is, the similarity of interacting pairs of individuals in certain attributes. The implication for Appalachia clearly seems to be that change agents should be as similar to their clients as possible. Yet an interesting paradox arises: "most change agents must try to communicate with clients who are much different than themselves in formal education, attitudes toward change, technical competence, and other attributes. In fact, if the clients did not differ from the change agent on these dimensions, the change agent would not have much of a role to play in the modernization process; the clients would already be as modern as the change agents" (Rogers 1969:182). However, one way to bridge the homophily-heterophily problem is to work through local opinion leaders. Schramm (1964:121) asserts that it is axiomatic that the change agent work with local leadership as a means of maintaining or increasing credibility, in addition to the more obvious utility of enlisting the considerable persuasive powers of such leaders.

Katz (1957) has postulated a two-step flow process by which mass media messages are received by "opinion leaders," who then pass on the information to everyday associates in whose eyes they are influential. The two-step flow model has proved to be valid only in specific instances and is not an acceptable general model. However, its emphasis upon the role of the opinion leader as a significant factor in the dissemination of information has been enormously useful. Further, Bostian (1970:115) hypothesizes that in developing areas and countries a two-step flow of information is more in evidence when locally relevant, instrumental, persuasive information is available via mass media. Yet, it remains uncertain to what extent opinion leaders actually perform a relay (or gatekeeper) function or an influence function with respect to new information. The influence function, of course, is assumed in the label "opinion leader," but information availability via mass media may create new gatekeepers, who may eventually become opinion leaders. As Rogers (1969:220) indicates, "It is strange that such an important topic (opinion leadership) has gone begging in modernization research."Indeed, opinion leadership is a key element in the design and implementation of communication strategies for modernization.

Rogers (1969:240) offers nine characteristics of opinion leaders (in contrast to their followers) which seem to hold true in both modern and traditional settings: (1) more formal education; (2) higher levels of literacy; (3) larger farms; (4) more agricultural and home innovativeness; (5) higher social status; (6) lower achievement motivation; (7) more exposure to mass media; (8) higher empathy; and (9) more political knowledge. That Rogers found opinion leaders in his study to exhibit lower achievement motivation should not be construed in any sense as a negation of the importance of this characteristic in modernization. In attempting to explain the finding, he suggests that opinion leaders perceive themselves as having "arrived" in terms of occupational excellence (Rogers 1969:227). In any event, the finding is derived from Rogers's Colombian data, and no further references are adduced either to explain such a finding or to support its cross-cultural validity.

Two variables for which differences are to be found with respect to traditional and modern settings are age and cosmopoliteness. It is a traditional belief that age brings wisdom (Lerner 1958:399). In a modern society, technical competence, social accessibility, and cosmopolite communication behavior usurp the place of age. Cosmopoliteness, more characteristic in the modern society of the opinion leader, is in the traditional setting often more characteristic of followers. This is consistent with the general notion that opinion leaders conform more closely to social system norms than followers.

It should be readily apparent that what one may expect to accomplish through an opinion leader in an Appalachian community will depend largely upon where that community lies along a continuum from traditional to modern. The more traditional communities of Appalachia have virtually no leadership. Weller (1966:44-49) talks of a pervading sense of fear in such communities which induces a reluctance to speak to others about matters on which a difference of opinion may exist, which in turn renders community decision making highly problematic. In such circumstances, it is not unusual for one's reference group to be confined to family members.

Nevertheless, many mountain communities possess so-called "mountain elites" (e.g., doctors, lawyers, teachers, businessmen) whose disproportionate influence in the community relative to their numbers suggests an additional important linkage with the larger society. Bowman and Plunkett (1969) conducted a study for the Economic Development Administration in which they sought to identify those elites who might best bridge the communication gaps both within the mountain area and between the mountains and the nation at large. Their findings did not specify whether the elites perform a gatekeeper or opinion leader function, but information was obtained which allows for some evaluation of the potential of mountain elites as "proselytizers for change." One of the more significant (and optimistic) conclusions regarding these elites was: "Even if migration claims large proportions of the more able, the area still contains substantial numbers of persons of apparent leadership potential who have spent time away from their homes, or who have left homes elsewhere to bring their experience to the mountains" (Bowman and Plunkett 1969:109).

The findings of Bowman and Plunkett also suggested a solid empathic foundation at the localite end so far as the potential cultural bridge role of mountain elites is concerned. Most of the respondents in the study identified strongly with the mountains, and high agreement also emerged in response to the statement "Mountain men are good workers if you understand how to get along with them" (Bowman and Plunkett 1969:123). This is encouraging in view of Lewis's (1970:11) contrasting assertion that "native colonizers" (native manufacturers and businessmen mainly in the coal mining areas) are even more disparaging in their evaluation of mountain people than are outsiders. However, at the cosmopolite end of the bridge, the foundation appeared less secure since large factions of local elites manifested resentment of outsiders and a defensiveness concerning local loyalties.

It would seem, therefore, that if government agencies and other change agents are to utilize fully the potential resources represented by the cultural bridge and opinion leader roles of the mountain elites, this localite defensiveness and resentment of outsiders must first be overcome. To do this, it is crucial that change agents eliminate inaccurate preconceptions and develop an empathic understanding and appreciation of mountain life. This condition will determine whether mountain leaders will exercise their considerable influence to facilitate or to hinder the dissemination of change information.

Not only does the mountainous terrain of the Appalachian region as a whole affect the mass media, hindering the transmission and reception of radio and television signals, but it is also a critical element affecting communication at the interpersonal level. Bowman and Plunkett (1969:99) indicate that many of the valley settlements are physically cut off from neighboring communities. This fosters cultural localist attitudes while impeding "development of the full mesh of 'nerve connections' that could serve to facilitate processes of modernization." In the case of such geographical isolation, these families have little contact with the outside world. Weller (1966:89) generalizes, "It is these families—isolated by distance, by lack of roads, and by choice—that most clearly display the characteristics of the folk culture." There have been studies of changes which occur in a village when a road links it with the rest of the world (Lerner 1958, Rao 1966). Pool (1966:99) states, "Nothing could be more revolutionary than a road." Quarles

(1955) provides an account of the effect of roads and highways on a community in Southern Appalachia as measured by a comparison of this community to a similar community in Appalachia without a highway network. Differentials included higher educational level, higher income, and more modern conveniences. Roads not only encourage the location of industry, but also facilitate personal contact and communication with urban centers, which in turn contribute to the introduction of modern norms, practices, and innovations.

INSTITUTIONAL CHANNELS OF COMMUNICATION

No discussion of the channels of communication within a society would be complete without some consideration of the various institutional channels. We have already discussed the effects of one type of institutional channel—the mass media. However, religious, governmental, economic, and educational institutions also serve as channels of information and as such are important potential carriers of modern norms, values, and practices. The most important channels in this respect, perhaps, are the educational institutions.

Schwarzweller and Brown (1969:6) make a strong case that educational institutions, "a natural and strategic center for the diffusion of urban or urbanizing norms," function as the major cultural bridge between relatively isolated Appalachian communities and larger American society. Conversely, the other major institutions, including the mass media, "are more insulated and have less direct, less strong, and less continuous lines of communication into the mountain region from the rest of American society."

This conclusion must certainly be tempered somewhat by noting the relative weakness of the Appalachian school systems, which are plagued by lack of funds, poor facilities, and low quality teachers. This situation led Donohew and Parker (1970), in a report on the impact of educational change in Appalachia, to conclude that even if Appalachian life styles and aspirations were to be changed, the institutional structure of education needed to support these aspirations would be inadequate.

Implicitly recognizing this weakness, Schwarzweller and Brown (1969:7) state that "the development of a strong, modern school system in the relatively isolated rural areas of this region will, in the long run, pay rich dividends in terms of linking these communities and their people—whether they remain in Appalachia or whether they chose to migrate to regions offering greater economic opportunity—into the mainstream of American Society." What is needed, then, is a greater effort at improving the Appalachian school system—not so much with respect to physical facilities as in terms of quality of teaching. The promise of the Appalachian school system as a major force for modernization is dependent upon this development.

DISCUSSION AND RECOMMENDATIONS

Modernization in Appalachia is essentially a communication process involving the dissemination and acceptance of the modern norms, values, and practices of larger American society. However, this process is hindered by the poverty of information which exists in Appalachia. Because of low levels of mass media availability, Appalachian residents experience relatively little contact with the normative, economic, and technological structures of modern society. Owing to the reciprocal effects of low media usage and low empathy, Appalachian people generally have little knowledge of the role requirements of a modern, urbanized society.

One of the consequences of this situation is that the awareness and acceptance of modern norms and practices necessary for the effective utilization of social services continue to be insufficient. Social programs will be much more viable in the context of a modernizing climate—a climate which can be provided only by the development of a modern, efficient, communication system involving the effective interaction of mass media, interpersonal, and institutional channels.

Such interaction of communication channels is also crucial in the day-to-day operation of service delivery programs. Service delivery agencies are necessarily highly and specifically mission-oriented, as, for instance, in such areas as family planning, health service, unemployment service, and AFDC. Such agencies and programs are also a major part of the change agent system. Given the specific mission-to-be-accomplished under any particular program, there are a host of interrelated questions concerning the basic processes of communication and modernization and concerning the extent and effectiveness of the information system for a given program. In planning and operating any program, one of the dangers is that an agency may be handicapped by its own special variety of informational poverty: administrators and staff may know relatively little about what sorts of communications (e.g., mass media, public meetings, word-of-mouth) have the greatest chances of performing successfully in their service area and with their target population. And without some systematic check (program evaluation), agency personnel may be relatively ignorant about what communications are working well. Since programs are ongoing, by definition and by practice, there is a continuing need to know many things about the service or target population as a basis for the successful maintenance of a communication program. Moreover, alternative communication models should be applied and evaluated as part of the general effort to demonstrate the best kind of service delivery model in particular localities.

More effort must also be directed toward working through existing communication facilities within Appalachia. One such project (Holloway 1970), planned and executed by the Institute for Public Broadcasting at Morehead State University, consisted of a thirteen-week adult radio program of continuing education for retired persons in a five-county area of eastern Kentucky and included a research (evaluative) component. More such projects aimed at subpopulations within Appalachia could prove invaluable.

RESEARCH NEEDS

There is a scarcity of studies concerned specifically with communication and modernization in Appalachia. Appalachia as a whole is similar in many ways to the developing countries; hence, examination of modernization literature directed toward these countries can be useful. Nevertheless, the differences between Appalachia and the developing nations should be continually borne in mind; the theoretical concepts which are ever-emerging in the modernization literature need to be tested for fit in a specifically Appalachian context.

Although the work of Donohew, Bowman and Plunkett, Stephens, and others cited in this chapter who have engaged in communication research in Appalachia has been extremely productive, a host of questions remains unanswered. Further research is needed, for example, in order to develop adequate conceptual models of the modernization process in Appalachia. Such models not only are essential to an understanding of the modernization process, but themselves help highlight the areas of need for further research. Another area in need of investigation is the interaction of mass media, interpersonal, cosmopolite, and

DANIEL E. JACO and PHILIP C. PALMGREEN

localite channels in the diffusion of innovations. Such research would be a valuable aid in discovering the mountain communication networks which carry essential information about programs and practices. A specific subarea which might be investigated is the communication and delivery of social services, with special emphasis upon client channel utilization.

Of interest also is the role of returning migrants in the communication nexus of Appalachia; what news do they bring back to the mountains about modern, urban society? We need not assume that it is necessarily positive. And to what extent are migrants more or less modern than those who remain? It may be that migrants are higher in media exposure and migrate as a result of relatively greater knowledge of economic and other opportunities in the outside world.

Although this listing of research questions is by no means exhaustive, it is representative of the types of questions which may be answered by future research into the relationships between communication and modernization in Appalachia. Out of such research may eventually emerge much of the vital "change technology" for bringing the traditional peoples of Appalachia out of poverty and isolation and into the prosperous mainstream of modern American society.

11 Poverty: A New Perspective

George L. Wilber

On the first page of this book the question was raised as to why the United States—the richest, best educated, most technically advanced nation in the world—is unable to eliminate poverty. As Alice Rivlin (1972:5) says, this is the most mystifying fact of our time. She points to a variety of "villain theories," the common element of which is that some identifiable group is believed to have the power to solve such problems as poverty but can't or won't. The villains include a wide variety of guilty persons, including the lazy, "good-for-nothing" low income groups, pot-smoking hippies, and left-wing agitators as well as "the establishment." Powerlessness theories contrast with the villain theories by making such social institutions as the government, business, organized labor, schools, and other institutional organizations the culprits, insisting that they block constructive solutions to poverty problems. Rivlin's alternative explanation, the conflicting objective theory, holds that we do not solve problems because we do not know how to do it.

In keeping with Rivlin's explanation, this book does not speak in terms of villains; emphasis has been on causes and processes, not as a means of placing blame but in order to explain why things happen. If there have been villains, they would include inadequate conceptualization and measurement, incomplete and sometimes shoddy hypotheses, and gaps in the substantive focus of specific research. In short, if villain there must be, then it might be identified as a lack of knowledge about the forces underlying poverty and the ways in which these forces operate to perpetuate poverty. Ignorance is not the only culprit, of course, but without knowledge and understanding, solutions to poverty appear quite hopeless.

In general, a primary strategy for research involves the formulation of a theory from which testable hypotheses may be derived, actually testing such hypotheses (and rival hypotheses), drawing tentative conclusions, revising the initial theory if necessary, and continuing to test hypotheses. As a first step this study provides a taxonomy of the properties (or dimensions or factors) of poverty and some isolated—certainly not comprehensive—propositions. Broad areas of needed research are also cited. In this final chapter, various aspects of the foregoing discussion are examined from three standpoints: the construction of poverty theory, measurements of variables, and the utility of research findings.

POVERTY THEORY CONSTRUCTION

Even among those most concerned with the problems of formally constructing theories, there is lack of agreement about the best way to proceed (Zetterberg 1965). Some prefer to begin with classifications and typologies and move toward a set of logically related propositions. Others inventory the literature in an effort to dredge up existing but sometimes vague and obscure propositions. Still others prefer to begin with abstract mathematical formulations. There is no one best or widely accepted method for constructing a theory. Many times the development of theory is haphazard and even inadvertent. In relatively rare instances (e.g., Blalock 1967) deliberate and systematic efforts to construct a theory are attempted.

As yet, there is no generally accepted theory of poverty, as we have noted in chapter 2. The task of constructing such a theory is handicapped by the fact that the term *poverty* is a common, everyday expression which is also used for slogan purposes. Despite legislative and program definitions (e.g., the Social Security Administration definition of poverty), the word has many meanings. But beyond the problems associated with the word itself, the many dimensions of the absence of resources and/or the inability to use resources to achieve an objective tend to be ignored or to be regarded as "correlates" of poverty.

For these kinds of reasons the initial step toward developing a program of poverty research was to conceptualize poverty as a *system* which possesses *properties*. The strategy for conceptualizing poverty in this way is essentially borrowed from measurement theory, according to which it is the properties of a system that are observable and measurable rather than the system itself. To those unaccustomed to the thinking and language of measurement theory it may seem awkward to talk of the properties of poverty. However, it is precision, theoretical support, and utility for research which are crucial to conceptualization rather than habit or popular usage.

By defining poverty as a relative lack of resources and/or inability to utilize resources, and by identifying basic kinds of resources, criteria are established by which properties of a poverty system can be identified. If this procedure were carried through to its ultimate conclusion (i.e., to a comprehensive listing of resources, mobilization processes, and poverty properties), quite a long list would result. The next steps are to posit relationships among these elements and to develop means of measuring the constructs or empirical reference.

In the actual conduct of research, and in test of causal models, it becomes necessary to work with very limited "middle range" theories which ultimately must be fitted into a coherent whole. A general strategy for application in a program of research: (1) takes a set of empirical generalizations and attempts to fill in gaps and introduce conceptual clarification; (2) attempts to explain particular phenomena by subsuming them under more general ones; and, (3) attempts to develop causal models of complex processes. The four kinds of steps toward theory construction identified by Blalock (1967:194-97) as a means of achieving these objectives are: (1) formulation of a schematic diagram, (2) narrowing the focus, (3) systematic statement and testing of alternative models, and (4) revision of the schematic diagram.

Formulation of a schematic diagram. Classes of variables that can be expected to influence the dependent variable(s) in question are blocked out first. A diagram for such a scheme may look very much like a causal scheme in which arrows run from one set of variables to another. Unlike a specific causal model the general schematic diagram represents only classes of variables. Figure 11.1 illustrates a scheme based on a few to the broad classes of individual and regional resources in which the central concern is to explain the education/skill level attained by individuals. In this particular example, three kinds of variables—social

FIGURE 11.1 Schematic Diagram with Blocks of Variables to Explain the Education/Skill Level of Individuals

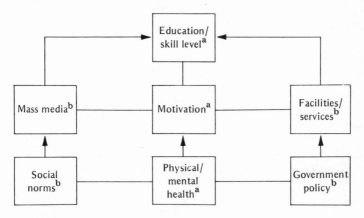

[a]Individual Characteristics
[b]Regional or society characteristics

norms, health, and government policy—are assumed to have direct influences on the mass media and community facilities and services as well as on the motivation of individuals. It is the second group of variables that are assumed to have a direct influence on the level of education and skill attained by an individual.

The schematic diagram can be useful in suggesting the kinds of variables that are potentially important enough to include in an empirical study. This framework itself is obviously not testable, but it does indicate possible causal connections. Once having sketched such a diagram, a specific study may be based on a few indicators within the classes of variables.

Narrowing the focus. It is often a practical impossibility to include in a single study all of the classes of variables and the several dimensions of such variables that are encompassed in a schematic diagram. It becomes a matter of discretion to specify exactly what is meant by such things as social norms, government policy, and motivation and to select specific measures of the variables to be included.

To follow the example suggested in Figure 11.1, in a study of educational/skill attainment, explanation of the level of attainment might require concentration on such questions as whether certain kinds

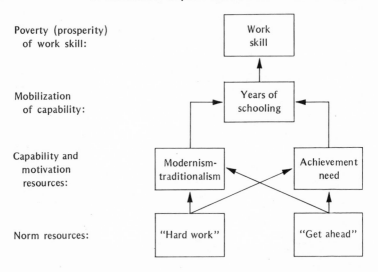

Poverty (prosperity)
of work skill:

Mobilization
of capability:

Capability and
motivation
resources:

Norm resources:

of social norms need to be understood and whether such norms influence motivation. At this point it will be necessary to become much
more specific about what is meant by norms, motivation, and level of
attainment. What are the norms relevant to "getting ahead," hard work,
and self-improvement? How are the degrees of modernism and need for
achievement dependent on such norms and how, in turn, do they
influence level of attainment? Figure 11.2 illustrates a relatively narrow
model derived from Figure 11.1. According to this model, the level of
work skill attained by an individual is influenced directly by the level of
his educational attainment, which in turn is a direct consequence of his
modernization and achievement-need motivations. These motivations
are further dependent on the norms of "hard work" and "getting
ahead." Notice that attributes of society (norms) are combined with
traits of individuals. This seemingly oversimplified model is in fact
highly complex. Not only are there five variables directly or indirectly
influencing the level of work skill, but there are possible interactions
and feedbacks among all the variables.

Systematic statement and testing of alternative models. In order to
make empirical predictions, it is necessary to measure a high proportion
of the variables in the general theoretical model. Also, it is necessary to

make a number of prior assumptions about linkages with unmeasured variables, measurement errors, and factors not included in the theory. For variables not included in the narrowed model, one can refer back to the general model—Figure 11.1, in our example. Quite obviously one could produce several models different from the one shown in Figure 11.2. To make a choice among these, one must question the relative ability of a specific model to explain what is going on. Only by adequate testing of alternative models can there be much assurance about a particular model.

Revision of schematic diagram. With the testing of several alternative models, the original scheme may be modified. Single classes of variables, or boxes, may be replaced by more complex formulations. Additional kinds of variables may need to be included. Specification of relationships over time may be desirable.

Preparing a schematic diagram is only a first step. Once variables have been selected, adequate measurement devices become crucial.

MEASUREMENT

Measurement problems are among the foremost difficulties in the conduct of poverty—and other—research. In chapter 3, discussion focused on problems in measuring poverty as it is defined officially. As indicated there, poverty was defined in terms of the adequacy of current family income to meet a constant, absolute standard of consumption, based on family size and farm versus nonfarm residence. Even if it is assumed that the Social Security Administration (SSA) definition of poverty is generally acceptable, there are numerous problems of measurement. National data are gathered annually on a cross-section sample of the population, which yields data on the incidence of poverty over time but does not contain the kinds of information necessary to trace individuals and families moving into or out of poverty. Measures currently in use also fail to reflect adequately the true extent of either absolute or relative deprivation.

Further, only three dimensions of the poverty systems—income, family size, and residence—are represented in the official indicator of poverty. With something less than total success in attempts to measure poverty under the relatively narrow SSA definition, one may question the wisdom of measuring even more numerous properties of the system of poverty. It is no secret that such problems are difficult, and the social sciences have been weak in solving problems of measurement. Nevertheless, sufficient headway has been made in recent years to afford promise of significant improvement in the measurement of variables. Measuring instruments and scales now cover a wide range of variables in the social sciences; and the technical know-how, especially among the younger generation of social scientists, to solve many of the measurement problems has improved. The outlook is therefore bright for developing and applying measures for such properties of the poverty system as modernism, need for achievement, social mobility, and social norms.

Essentially, more and better measures of such general and abstract variables as the economic system, social norms, frustration, and the effectiveness of community services are needed. As indicators, measures may be distinguished by whether they are primarily designed and employed to trace trends and identify patterns as with a cost-of-living index or whether they serve as surrogates for abstract concepts in multivariate analytical models as with an index of socioeconomic status. In either case, indicators provide information relevant to a system, such as the poverty system. Indicators should have the capacity to be aggregated or disaggregated to levels appropriate to the system of interest. Measures which currently are called "social indicators" usually contain social account or bookkeeping kinds of information. In the more traditional sense, indicators are used in research as measures of something unobservable; that is, two or more research indicators are typically employed in an effort to explain why something is happening. Relationships among such indicators and between them and what they supposedly measure are of fundamental importance in research. Consequently, measures of poverty properties are extremely important.

This is not the opportune time nor place to elaborate in detail the kinds of measures needed nor how such measures should be developed and applied. Earlier chapters dealt with some specific measurement problems, for example, modernism, need for achievement, poverty of information, childbearing, family planning, and migration. There are obvious gaps in the taxonomy of the poverty system presented earlier and in the variables in need of measurement. Health, housing, job training, special problems of youth and the aged, drug abuse, crime and delinquency, and others were treated lightly or not at all in the earlier discussion.

Health problems, for instance, are widely recognized as barriers to independence and self-support. Yet the measures of health are largely the presence or absence of an illness, disease, or impairment. There are no readily available measures of the degree of "good health." Under-employment is another instance of a commonly accepted barrier to an escape from poverty. What does it mean and how can it be measured? Seemingly, it can mean employment below a person's skill level and/or employment for "too short" a period of time. Weeks and hours worked can be determined rather easily, but just when are people working below their skill level? The use of drugs or alcohol can interfere with and curb a person's activity to the extent that he loses his job, his family, and his house. The relativity of such actions and their results are abundantly clear. Yet, as noted in the third chapter, measures of poverty in use today fail to account for relative deprivation. That is, values, attitudes, and behavior standards change over time; what might have been "overconsumption" of drugs at one time may be treated as normal at another.

RESEARCH UTILIZATION

The value of research is judged from various standards and points of view. In the community of scholars, the obvious standard of scientific quality is almost invariably applied, but even experts sometimes disagree about logical, theoretical, and methodological aspects of a given piece of research. A second standard is the utility of research results. For whom and for what purpose(s) are the results useful? Much has been written—and discussions are likely to continue in the future—about these two questions. In any research project or program, these questions underlie the research operation. The object in raising the issue here is that both kinds of questions must be considered in present-day research.

It is possible to identify two major groups, each with a strong interest in one of the questions as opposed to the other: (1) scientists and scholars and (2) change agents. The first group traditionally has been concerned with knowledge for its own sake. Research results are judged largely on the grounds of their contribution to the body of knowledge. This contribution is often evaluated by theoretical and methodological standards. The immediate applicability of findings to problems of society is typically a secondary concern at best.

In contrast, for change agents the interest in research focuses on the application of results to help solve some practical problem. The term "change agents" is used here to include policy makers, planners, and administrators at the top levels of federal governmental operation and at state and local levels. Change agents would also include "workers" who are responsible for implementing policies and programs. Most of this rather heterogeneous group has little concern with the theoretical or scientific importance of research findings, and members of it may indeed view this type of evaluation as a nuisance or a necessary evil. The central and overriding question for change agents is whether the findings are immediately useful for the particular problems or programs in which they are involved. If poverty, for instance, is their business, then only that research which provides answers and directions for the immediate reduction of poverty problems is relevant to them. Much the same is true for those concerned with the practical problems of health, unemployment, and housing, or with the needs of the aged.

Unfortunately there is a mission-orientation conflict of interest, especially between the extremists from either group. Yet there is ample evidence that currently most organized research is supported by mission-oriented agencies, and it appears likely that during the decade of the 1970s this pattern will continue. Consequently, the burden is on researchers to demonstrate the utility of research findings for action agencies. Researchers must show how results of their work can be used, who can use them, and what the results of such utilization may be.

One result is that the mission of a sponsoring agency must be an integral part of research. That is, from the formulation of a research problem through analysis and conclusions, research must be designed and executed with the interests of the mission in mind. Researchers have a moral obligation to point out pitfalls and alternative courses of action and to offer policy recommendations; sponsoring agencies have a corresponding obligation to listen and heed such cautions and suggestions. In the final analysis, those who pay the bill will largely determine research objectives, while the researcher must produce results.

In addition to setting research objectives consistent with program objectives and insisting on useful results, sponsoring agencies have a legitimate interest in manipulable variables, as mentioned in chapter 2. More specifically, an agency with a highly specific mission—defined by legislation and administrative policies and practices—is necessarily concerned with variables which are potentially manipulable and relevant to the specific mission, and to that mission only. For example, although the variables color and sex cannot be manipulated in a program to influence change, some individual characteristics associated with color or sex can be modified; for example, educational and employment opportunities for black women can be increased.

Research can meet the mission-requirements of sponsoring agencies by conducting studies of groups and individuals being served by the agency. Thus, farmers and farm laborers are appropriate subjects for research sponsored by the Department of Agriculture. Welfare recipients are suitable subjects for Social and Rehabilitation Service research, and wage earners, for studies requested by the Department of Labor. Despite an apparent neatness in this kind of division, there are many gray areas in which some groups might be subjects of overlapping studies while others could possibly be overlooked completely.

More fundamentally important from a research standpoint, however, is the problem of making inferences or reaching conclusions based on observations of restricted segments of the universe. How, for example, can meaningful conclusions be drawn about income and occupational questions by looking only at agricultural workers? How can sensible conclusions be reached about motivation to work by studying only welfare recipients? How can defensible conclusions about social mobility be reached by looking only at industrial wage earners? The answer seems clear that mission-action agencies should not be overly myopic by considering exclusively their own specific target groups. Obviously they require knowledge about their clients but for adequate evaluation of their own programs they really need information on a far broader basis.

Nevertheless, research based in mini-theories can be worthwhile for the researcher and the action agency. Let us explore briefly a hypothetical study design for an investigation of AFDC-WIN mothers. Suppose we are concerned with AFDC-WIN mothers and the problems of helping them have fewer children and becoming self-supporting at a level above the official poverty threshold. General objectives are: (a) to explain why they have the number of children they have; (b) to explain why they fail to be self-supporting; and, (c) to develop an information base for the effective operation of a program intended to curb their fertility and help them become self-supporting. The ideal is to account for all factors that might affect the outcomes, but realistically only a limited number of all possible influences can be handled at any one

FIGURE 11.3 Model to Explain Fertility and Employment of
AFDC-WIN Mothers

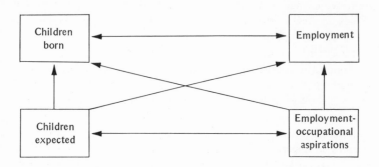

time. Suppose further that a resource-mobilization model is selected as the basic theoretical-analytical tool.

As an initial effort, two propositions are formulated:

1. The number of children born is a function of the number of children expected (or desired) by AFDC-WIN mothers.

2. The employment of AFDC-WIN mothers is a function of their employment-occupational aspirations.

Each of these two bivariate propositions could be evaluated rather easily, given the basic raw data for the variables involved. In both instances it is very likely that the hypothesized independent influences would account for only a small amount of the variance. Also, it is likely that fertility and employment are interrelated. Therefore, the initial propositions can be modified:

1a. The number of children born is a function of the number of children expected, the employment status, and employment-occupational aspirations.

2a. The employment of AFDC-WIN mothers is a function of their employment-occupational aspirations, the number of children born, and the number of children expected.

Diagrammatically, combining the two statements we have the relationships shown in Figure 11.3, where the presence and direction of an arrow represents hypothesized influences. With four variables there are six possible pair-wise connections, and if each of these interconnections is examined while controlling for a third variable there are an additional twelve relationships. Little imagination is required to see that the

174   GEORGE L. WILBER

addition of another variable increases the complexity of such a model.

Nevertheless, curiosity drives us to inquire about things that might influence fertility and employment through their impact on expectations and aspirations. On the basis of general information the following proposition is set forth:

3. Both the number of children expected and employment-occupational aspirations are dependent on (a) educational attainment, (b) acceptance of a norm to "get ahead," (c) exposure to information about family planning services, (d) a strong need for achievement, and (e) access to and utilization of employment counseling.

This statement, diagrammed in Figure 11.4, extends the model by inquiring into factors that potentially influence the number of children expected and employment-occupational aspirations. Figures 11.3 and 11.4 could be combined into a single model.

This illustration shows that some semblance of a theory can be utilized to explain specific behaviors and attitudes among the clients of a particular action program. Hence, the interests of both the researcher and the action agency can be satisfied in a single research operation.

Attention has been directed to the question of how research can be planned, designed, and executed to satisfy the interest of both the researcher and his mission-oriented sponsor. Yet there is another side of the research-utilization question which should not be ignored. It is important that the findings of all research—whether sponsored or not—be communicated to those in action programs who can in fact make use of the results. Until rather recently there has been little effort concentrated in this direction. Researchers customarily publish reports—often unintelligible to a layman—and occasionally talk with change agents. Change agents have often been too busy and too confused by research to make a deliberate effort to use the results. The consequences of such breakdowns in communication are far too serious for this situation to continue unchanged. Over the next decade or two it should be interesting to watch activities directed toward more effective presentation and dissemination of research findings to those in a position to use them toward the solution of practical problems.

A FINAL NOTE

As a mark of the times, this book represents an effort to blend a number of ingredients, to present a variety of thoughts and experiences

FIGURE 11.4   Model to Explain Expected Fertility & Employment Aspirations of AFDC-WIN Mothers

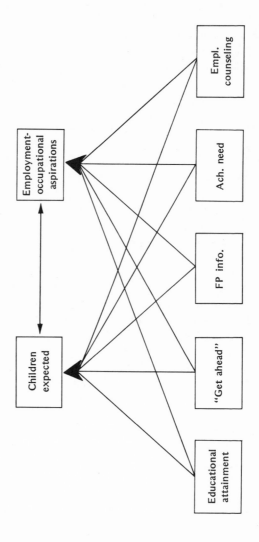

concerning the topic of poverty. Beginning with a general and still rather crude taxonomy of poverty properties, the discussion focused on development of models stemming from this initial taxonomy, problems of measurement, some specific facets of poverty, and suggested research needs.

A number of needs become apparent:

1. There is a need for an interdisciplinary approach to poverty. Poverty problems overlap; to attempt a narrow single-discipline approach is to risk oversimplification of the extent to which poverty affects the lives of the needy.

2. An adequate theory of poverty must be developed to serve as a framework for a long-term program of research.

3. The current poverty-knowledge base is extremely flimsy; this relative ignorance impedes practical solutions to poverty problems.

4. Research results should be oriented not only to the usual academic standards of methodology and theory; of equal importance is research geared to utilization in action programs.

The ultimate conclusion appears to be that, unless research efforts are redoubled, particularly in those projects which can result in immediate implementation, the numbers of those suffering from the various properties of poverty will continue to increase relentlessly.

References

Agocs, Carol
   1970.   Social indicators: selected readings. *Annals of the American Academy of Political and Social Service* 388(March):127-32.
Allen, Vernon, ed.
   1970.   *Psychological factors in poverty.* Chicago: Markham.
Appalachia.
   1970.   A Tennessee district helps a rural county plan future development. 3(February):16-22.
   1971.   4(February):9-10.
Aronson, E.
   1958.   The need for achievement as measured by graphic expression. In *Motives in fantasy, action, and society,* ed. J. W. Atkinson. Princeton, N.J.: Van Nostrand.
Atkinson, J. W.
   1955.   The achievement motive and recall of interrupted and completed tasks. In *Studies in motivation,* ed. D. C. McClelland. New York: Appleton-Century-Crofts.
   1966.   Motivation determinants of risk-taking behavior. In *A theory of achievement motivation,* ed. J. W. Atkinson and N. T. Feather. New York: Wiley.
Atkinson, J. W., and Litwin, G. H.
   1966.   Achievement motive and text anxiety conceived as motive to approach success and motive to avoid failure. In *A theory of*

achievement motivation, ed. J. W. Atkinson and N. T. Feather. New York: Wiley.

Barkan, Barry, and Lloyd, R. Baldwin.
  1970. Picking poverty's pocket. *Mountain Life and Work* 46 (September): 4-9, 19-21.

Battle, Esther S., and Rotter, J. B.
  1963. Children's feelings of personal control as related to social class and ethnic group. *Journal of Personality* 31(December):945-59.

Bauer, Raymond A.
  1964. The obstinate audience: The influence process from the point of view of social communication. *American Psychologist* 19:319-28.

Beasley, Joseph D.
  1967. The United States: The Orleans Parish family planning demonstration program. *Studies in Family Planning* 25 (December): 5-9.

Behavorial Science Center, Sterling Institute.
  1969. *Proposal for a training of neighborhood workers, mid-level supervisors and senior staff in eleven CAAs in the Kentucky District,* (REP MA-70-1). Washington, D.C.: Office of Economic Opportunity.

Belcher, John C.
  1962. Population growth and characteristics. In *The southern Appalachian region: A survey,* ed. Thomas Ford, pp. 37-53. Lexington: University of Kentucky Press.

Berelson, B.
  1964. National family planning programs: A guide. *Studies in Family Planning* 5 (December): 1-12.

Berelson, B., ed.
  1965. *Family planning and population programs.* Chicago: University of Chicago Press.

Birren, James E., and Hess, Robert E.
  1968. Influences of biological, physiological, and social deprivations upon learning and performance. *Perspectives on Human Deprivation* 89-183.

Blake, Judith.
  1966. Ideal family size among white Americans: A quarter of a century's evidence. *Demography* 3 (no.1):154-73.

REFERENCES

1967a. Family size in the 1960s—a baffling fad. *Eugenics Quarterly* 14 (March):60-74.

1967b. Parental control, delayed marriage, and population policy. In *Proceedings of the World Population Conference, 1965*, vol. 2, United Nations.

1967c. Reproductive ideals and educational attainment among white Americans, 1943-1960. *Population Studies* 21 (September):159-74.

Blalock, Hubert M., Jr.

1961. *Causal inferences in nonexperimental research*. New York: Wiley.

1967. *Toward a theory of minority-group relations*. New York: Wiley.

1969. *Theory construction: From verbal to mathematical formulations*. Englewood Cliffs, N.J.: Prentice-Hall.

Blau, P. M.

1967. *Exchange and power in social life*. New York: Wiley.

Blau, P. M., and Duncan, O. D.

1967. *The American occupational structure*. New York: Wiley.

Bogue, Donald J.

1968. Acceptance of a family planning program by the rural poor: Summary of an experiment in Alabama. In *Rural poverty in the United States*, ed. C. E. Bishop and G. L. Wilber, chap. 22. Washington, D.C.: Government Printing Office.

1969. *Principles of demography*. New York: Wiley.

1971. Policies for overcoming rural resistance to family planning. Paper presented at the annual meeting of the Rural Sociological Society, Denver, Colorado. (Mimeographed)

Bogue, Donald J., ed.

1966. *The rural south fertility experiments: report number 1*. Chicago: Community and Family Study Center, University of Chicago.

1967. *Sociological contributions to family planning research*. Chicago Community and Family Study Center, University of Chicago.

Bogue, Donald J., and Hagood, Margaret Jarman

1953. *Subregional migration in the United States, 1935-1940*, vol. 2, *Differential migration in the corn and cotton belts*. Oxford, Ohio: Scripps Foundation.

Bostian, Lloyd R.

　1970.　The two-step flow theory: Cross-cultural implications. *Journalism Quarterly* 47 (Spring):109-17.

Bowles, Gladys K., and Tarver, James D.

　1965.　*Net migration of the population, 1950-60 by age, sex, and color,* vol. 2, *Analytical groupings of U.S. counties.* U.S. Department of Agriculture. Washington, D.C.: Government Printing Office.

Bowman, Mary Jean, and Plunkett, H. Dudley.

　1969.　*Communication and mountain development: A summary of two East Kentucky studies.* U.S. Department of Commerce. Economic Development Administration.

Branscome, James.

　1971.　Appalachian migrants and the need for a national policy. *Appalachia* 4(February):4-8.

Brody, Eugene B., ed.

　1969.　*Behavior in new environments: Adaptation of migrant populations.* Beverly Hills, Calif.: Sage Publications.

Brown, James S., and Hillery, George A., Jr.

　1962.　The great migration, 1940-1960. In *The southern Appalachian region: A survey,* ed. Thomas R. Ford, pp. 54-78. Lexington: University of Kentucky Press.

Brown, Roger.

　1965.　*Social psychology.* New York: Free Press.

Bumpass, Larry.

　1969.　Age at marriage as a variable in socio-economic differentials in fertility. *Demography* 6(February):45-54.

Burlage, Robb K.

　1970.　Toward a people's ARC. *Peoples' Appalachia* 1 (August/September):5-7.

Byrne, Donn.

　1966.　*An introduction to personality: A research approach.* Englewood Cliffs, N.J.: Prentice-Hall.

Cain, Stephen R.

　1968.　A selective description of a Knox County mountain neighborhood. Unit 3 of a report from a study of an OEO community action program in Knox County, Kentucky, by an interdisciplinary team of the University of Kentucky, 1965-68.

Campbell, Arthur A.
  1968. The role of family planning in the reduction of poverty. *Journal of Marriage and the Family* 30 (May):236-45.
  1969. Family planning and the five million. *Family Planning Perspectives* 1(October):33-36.
Carlin, Tom A.
  1971. Economic analysis of the predicted effects of alternative family assistance programs on selected household expenditures. Ph.D. diss. Pennsylvania State University.
Caudill, Harry M.
  1962. *Night comes to the Cumberlands.* Boston: Atlantic, Little, and Brown.
Caudill, Morris K.
  1968. The youth development program. Unit 6 of a report from a study of an OEO community action program in Knox County, Kentucky, by an interdisciplinary team of the University of Kentucky, 1965-68.
Chu, Godwin C.
  1968. The impact of mass media on a gemeinschaft-like social structure. *Rural Sociology* 33(June):189-99.
Clark, Faith.
  1969. The 1965-66 food consumption survey: scope, methodology, and highlights. In *Using Food Surveys in Consumer Education,* pp. 43-56. Raleigh, N.C.: Agriculture Policy Institute.
Coll, Blanche D.
  1969. *Perspectives in public welfare: A history.* Washington, D.C.: U.S. Department of Health, Education, and Welfare.
Commission on Population Growth and the American Future.
  1971. *Population growth and America's future; An interim report.* Washington, D.C.: Government Printing Office.
  1972. *Population and the American future: The report of the Commission.* Washington, D.C.: Government Printing Office.
Coombs, Lolagene C., and Freedman, Ronald.
  1970. Pre-marital pregnancy, childspacing and later economic achievement. *Population Studies* 24(November):389-412.
Corkey, Elizabeth C.
  1964. A family planning program for the low income family. *Journal of Marriage and the Family* 26(November):478-80.

Corsa, Leslie.
  1968. United States: Public policy and programs in family planning. *Studies in Family Planning* 27 (March): 1- 4.
Cowgill, Donald O.
  1963. Transition theory as general population theory. *Social Forces* 41(March):270-74.
Cox, F. N.
  1962. An assessment of the achievement behavior system in children. *Child Development* 33:907-16.
DeJong, Gordon F.
  1965. Religious fundamentalism, socio-economic status, and fertility attitudes in the Southern Appalachians. *Demography* 2:540-48.
  1968. *Appalachian fertility decline: A demographic and sociological analysis.* Lexington: University of Kentucky Press.
Deutschmann, Paul J.
  1963. The mass media in an underdeveloped village. *Journalism Quarterly* 40 (Winter): 27-35.
Deutschmann, Paul J., Ellingsworth, Huber, and McNelly, John T.
  1968. *Communication and social change in Latin America.* New York: Praeger.
Doherty, Neville.
  1970. *Rurality, poverty, and health.* Agricultural Economic Report no. 172, Economic Research Service, USDA. Washington, D.C.: U.S. Department of Agriculture.
Donohew, Lewis.
  1967. Communication and readiness for change in Appalachia. *Journalism Quarterly* 44 (Winter):679-87.
Donohew, Lewis, and Parker, Joanne M.
  1970. *Impacts of educational change: Efforts in Appalachia.* Las Cruces, New Mexico: Clearinghouse on Rural Education and Small Schools, New Mexico State University.
Donohew, Lewis, and Singh, B. Krishna.
  1969. Communication and life styles in Appalachia. *Journal of Communication* 19:202-16.
Donohew, Lewis, and Thorp, Robert.
  1966. Mass media availability patterns in Kentucky counties. Communications Research Monograph no. 1, School of Communications, University of Kentucky.

Duncan, O. D.
    1965.   Farm background and differential fertility. *Demography* 2:240-49.
Easterlin, Richard A.
    1973.   Does money buy happiness? *The Public Interest* (Winter):3-10.
Eldridge, Hope T.
    1964.   A cohort approach to the analysis of migration differentials. *Demography* 1:212-19.
Fairchild, Charles K.
    1970.   *Worker relocation: A review of U.S. Department of Labor mobility demonstration projects.* Washington, D.C.: Shelley.
Ford, Thomas R.
    1964.   *Health and demography in Kentucky.* Lexington: University of Kentucky Press.
Ford, Thomas R., and DeJong, Gordon F.
    1963.   The decline of fertility in the Southern Appalachian mountain region. *Social Forces* 43 (October):89-96.
Forward, J. R., and Williams, J. R.
    1970.   Internal-external control and black militancy. *Journal of Social Issues* 26:75-92.
Foster, George M.
    1962.   *Traditional cultures and the impact of technological change.* New York: Harper & Row.
    1965.   Peasant society and the image of limited good. *American Anthropologist* 67:293-315.
    1969.   *Applied anthropology.* Boston: Little, Brown.
Foster, Phillips, and Yost, Larry.
    1969.   Uganda: Population growth and rural development. *Studies in Family Planning* 43 (June):1-6.
Freedman, Deborah.
    1963.   The relation of economic status to fertility. *American Economic Review* 53(June): 414-26.
Freedman, Marcia K., and Wagner, John, Jr.
    1965.   Programs and services to aid the integration of rural youth in urban communities. In *Rural youth in crisis: Facts, myths, and social change,* ed. Lee G. Burchinal, pp. 309-25. Washington, D.C.: U.S. Dept. of Health, Education, and Welfare.

Freedman, Ronald.
   1965. Transition from high to low fertility: Challenge to demographers. *Population Index* 31 (October):417-29.
   1967. Applications of the behavorial sciences to family planning programs. *Studies in Family Planning* 33 (October):5-9.

Freedman, Ronald, and Coombs, L.
   1966a. Childspacing and family economic position. *American Sociological Review* 31(October):631-48.
   1966b. Economic considerations in family growth decisions. *Population Studies* 20(November):197-222.

Fuchs, Lawrence H.
   1967. The role and communication task of the change agent—experiences of the peace corps volunteers in the Philippines. In *Communication and change in the developing countries,* ed. Daniel Lerner and Wilbur Schramm, pp. 235-78. Honolulu: East-West Center Press.

Fuchs, Victor R.
   1969. Comment on measuring the low income population. In *Six papers on the sized distribution of wealth and income,* ed. Lee Soltow, p. 200. New York: National Bureau of Economic Research.

Grabill, Wilson H., Kiser, Clyde V., and Whelpton, Pascal K.
   1958. *The fertility of American women.* New York: Wiley.

Hall, Edward T.
   1959. *The silent language.* New York: Doubleday.
   1966. *The hidden dimension.* New York: Doubleday.

Halloran, James.
   1970. Mass media in society: The need of research. UNESCO Research Report.

Hamilton, C. Horace.
   1958. Educational selectivity of rural-urban migration: Preliminary results of a North Carolina study. In *Selected Studies of Migration since World War II,* pp. 116-22. New York: Milbank Memorial Fund.

Hansen, Niles.
   1970. *Rural poverty and the urban crisis.* Bloomington: Indiana University Press.

Harkavy, Oscar, Jaffe, Frederick S., and Wishik, Samuel M.
    1969.   Family planning and public policy: Who is misleading whom? *Science* 165(July 29):367-73.

Harris, T. George.
    1971.   To know why men do what they do: A conversation with David C. McClelland. *Psychology Today* 4(January):35-39, 70-75.

Hathaway, Dale E., Beegle, J. Allen, and Bryant, W. Keith.
    1968.   *People of rural America.* A 1960 Census Monograph. Washington, D.C.: Government Printing Office.

Heckhausen, Heinz.
    1968.   Achievement motive research: Current problems and some contributions towards a general theory of motivation. In *Nebraska symposium on motivation*, ed. William J. Arnold. Lincoln: University of Nebraska Press.

Hollister, Robinson G., and Palmer, John L.
    1969.   *The impact of inflation on the poor.* Madison: Institute for Research on Poverty, University of Wisconsin.

Holloway, Donald F.
    1970.   *An adult radio project for cultural, recreational and area development in Eastern Kentucky.* Annual Project Report, Morehead (Ky.) State University.

Inkeles, Alex.
    1966.   The modernization of man. In *Modernization*, ed. Myron Weiner. New York: Basic Books.

Jaffe, Frederick S.
    1964.   Family planning and poverty. *Journal of Marriage and the Family* 26 (November): 467-70.
    1967.   The United States: A strategy for implementing family planning services. *Studies in Family Planning* 17 (February):5-12.
    1971.   Estimating the need for subsidized family planning services. *Family Planning Perspectives* 3(January):51-55.

Jaffe, Frederick S., ed.
    1967.   *Rural family planning programs.* New York: Planned Parenthood-World Population.

Jaffe, Frederick S., and Guttmacher, Alan F.
    1968.   Family planning programs in the United States. *Demography* 5:910-23.

Johnson, Cyrus M., Coleman, A. Lee, and Clifford, William B.
    1967.   Mountain families in poverty. RS-29, University of Kentucky, Department of Sociology. (Mimeographed)

Kahl, Joseph A.
    1967.   Modern values and fertility ideas in Brazil and Mexico. *Journal of Social Issues* 23(October):99-114.
    1968.   *The measurement of modernism: A study of values in Brazil and Mexico.* Austin, Texas: University of Texas.

Katz, Elihu.
    1957.   The two-step flow of communication: An up-to-date report on an hypothesis. *Public Opinion Quarterly* 21:61-78.

Katz, Elihu, and Lazarsfeld, Paul F.
    1955.   *Personal influence.* Glencoe, Ill.: Glencoe Free Press.

Keller, Alan B., Sims, John H., Henry, William E.,
    and Crawford, Thomas J.
    1970.   Psychological sources of resistance to family planning. *Merrill-Palmer Quarterly* 16(July): 286-302.

Klapper, Joseph.
    1960.   *The effects of mass communication.* New York: Free Press.

Kolb, D. A.
    1965.   Achievement motivation training for under-achieving high-school boys. *Journal of Personality and Social Psychology* 2:783-92.

Kosa, John, Antonovskv, Aaron and Zola, Irving K.
    1969.   *Poverty and Health.* Cambridge: Harvard University Press.

Land, Kenneth C.
    1971.   On the definition of social indicators. *American Sociologist* 6(November):322-25.

Lansing, John B., and Dickinson, Katherine.
    1970.   *Consumption patterns of the poor.* Working paper from OEO, *Study of Family Income Dynamics* (August). Ann Arbor: Survey Research Center, University of Michigan.

Lee, Everett S.
    1966.   A theory of migration. *Demography* 3(no.1):47-57.

Lefcourt, H. M.
    1966.   Internal versus external control of reinforcement: A review. *Psychological Bulletin* 65:206-20.

Lerner, Daniel.
  1958. *The passing of traditional society.* Glencoe, Ill.: Glencoe Free
        Press.
  1963. Toward a communication theory of modernization. In *Com-
        munications and political development,* ed. Lucien W. Pye,
        pp. 327-50. Princeton: Princeton University Press.
  1967. Communication and the prospects of innovative develop-
        ment. In *Communication and change in the developing
        countries,* ed. Daniel Lerner and Wilbur Schramm, pp.
        305-17. Honolulu: East-West Center Press.
Lerner, Monroe.
  1969. Social differences in physical health. In *Poverty and health,*
        ed. John Kosa, pp. 69-112. Cambridge.: Harvard University
        Press.
Lewis, Helen.
  1970. Fatalism in the coal industry. *Mountain Life and Work* (Jan-
        uary):4-15.
Lewis, Oscar.
  1966. *LaVida: Puerto Rican family in the culture of poverty—San
        Juan and New York.* New York: Random House.
Lionberger, Herbert F.
  1960. *Adoption of new ideas and practices.* Ames: Iowa State
        University Press.
Lippitt, Ronald, Watson, Jeanne, and Westley, Bruce.
  1958. *The dynamics of planned change.* New York: Harcourt,
        Brace, and World.
Lipset, S. M., and Bendix, R.
  1959. *Social mobility in industrial society.* Berkeley: University of
        California Press.
Loomis, Charles P.
  1959. Tentative types of directed social change involving systemic
        linkage. *Rural Sociology* 24(December):383-90.
Losman, Donald.
  1970. The nature of Appalachian unemployment. *Appalachia*
        3(April):25-27.
MacDonald, A. P., Jr.
  1970. Internal-external locus of control and the practice of birth
        control. *Psychological Reports* 27:206.

REFERENCES   189

1971. Internal-external locus of control: A promising rehabilitation variable. *Journal of Counseling Psychology* 18:111-16.

Madden, J. P., Pennock, J. L., and Jaeger, C. M.
1968. Equivalent levels of living: A new approach to scaling the poverty lines to different family characteristics and place of residence. In *Rural poverty in the United States,* p. 545. Washington, D.C.: Government Printing Office.

Madden, J. Patrick.
1970. Social change and public policy in rural America: Data and research needs for the 1970s. *American Journal of Agricultural Economics* 52(May):308-14.

Malzberg, B., and Lee, Everett S.
1956. *Migration and mental disease.* New York: Social Science Research Council.

McClelland, D. C.
1961. *The achieving society.* Princeton, N.J.: Van Nostrand.

McClelland, D. C., and Winter, D. G.
1969. *Motivating economic achievement.* New York: Free Press.

McNelly, John T., and Molina, Julio.
1972. Communication, stratification and international affairs information in a developing urban society. *Journalism Quarterly* 49 (Summer): 316-26.

Miller, Herman P.
1966. *Income distribution in the United States.* Washington, D.C.: U.S. Bureau of the Census, Government Printing Office.

Miller, S. M., Rein, Martin, Roby, Pamela, and Gross, Bertran M.
1967. Poverty, inequality and conflict. *Annals of the Academy of Political and Social Science* 337(September):16.

Murray, H. A.
1938. *Explorations in personality.* New York: Science Editions (1962).

Myers, Phineas Barton.
1959. *Ninety years after Lincoln.* New York: Exposition Press.

National Advisory Commission on Rural Poverty.
1967. *The people left behind.* Washington, D.C.: Government Printing Office.

Nixon, Richard M.
1969. *Presidential Message on Population, July 18.*

REFERENCES

O'Connor, R. W., Allen, David T., and Smith, Jack C.
  1969.   United States: Information flow and service-oriented feed-
           back in family planning programs. *Studies in Family Planning*
           46 (October):6-10.
Odegaard, O.
  1932.   Emigration and insanity. *Acta Psychiatrica et Neurologria,
           Supplement 4.*
Office of Economic Opportunity.
  1968.   *Need for subsidized family planning services: United States:
           Each state and county.* New York: A report produced by
           Center for Family Planning Program Development, The
           Technical Assistance Division, Planned Parenthood-World
           Population.
Orshansky, Mollie.
  1963.   Children of the poor. *Social Security Bulletin* 26(July).

Panko, Thomas R., ed.
  1969.   *Research in adaptation of migrants.* Report of a Conference.
           Atlanta: Southern Regional Education Board.

Perkin, Gordon W.
  1969a. Measuring clinic performance. *Family Planning Perspectives*
           1(Spring):36-38.
  1969b. Pregnancy prevention in "high risk" women: A strategy for
           new national family planning programs. *Studies in Family
           Planning* 44(August):19-24.
Peterson, William.
  1969.   *Population.* London: Macmillan.

Planned Parenthood Federation of America.
  1967.   *Five million women.* New York: Planned Parenthood-World
           Population.
Polgar, Steven.
  1966.   United States: the PPFA Mobile Service Project in New York
           City. *Studies in Family Planning* 15 (October): 9-15.

Pool, Ithiel de Sola.
  1966.   Communication and development. In *Modernization: The
           dynamics of growth,* ed. Myron Weiner, pp. 98-109. New
           York: Basic Books.
Population Reference Bureau.
  1965.   The emerging concensus: The courts, the Congress, and the

Administration move toward a United States population policy. *Population Bulletin* 21(August):51-71.

1970.   Population developments in 1970. *Population Bulletin* 26(December): 1-25.

Potter, Harry R., Gowty, Willis J., and Larson, Calvin J.

1969.   Poverty in rural America: The situation in an "average income county." Paper presented to the Rural Sociological Society Annual Meeting, San Francisco, California, (August 28-31).

President's Commission on Income Maintenance Programs.

1969.   *Poverty amid plenty—American paradox.* Washington, D.C.: Government Printing Office.

Price, Daniel O.

1965.   A mathematical model for migration suitable for simulation on an electronic computer. In *International Population Conference Proceedings*, pp. 665-73. Vienna: International Union for the Scientific Study of Population.

Quarles, Mary A.

1955.   When roads come. *Mountain Life and Work* 31(Spring): 40-43.

Rainwater, Lee.

1960.   *And the poor get children.* Chicago: Quadrangle Books.

Rao, Y. V. Lakshmana.

1966.   *Communication and development: A study of two Indian villages.* Minneapolis: University of Minnesota Press.

Ravenstein, E. G.

1885.   The laws of migration. *Journal of the Royal Statistical Society* 48, pt. 2 (June):167-235.

1889.   The laws of migration. *Journal of the Royal Statistical Society* 52(June):241-305.

Redfield, Robert.

1956.   *Peasant society and culture.* Chicago: University of Chicago Press.

Reimanis, G.

1970.   *A study of home environment and readiness for achievement at school.* Final Report, Project No. 9-B-065, Grant No. OEG-2-420065-1036, United States Department of Health, Education and Welfare. Office of Education, Bureau of Research.

Reynolds, Jack.
  1970. Delivering family planning services: Autonomous vs. integrat-
         ed clinics. *Family Planning Perspectives* 2(January):15-22.
Richardson, Russell H.
  1969. Family planning in the southeastern United States. *Family
         Planning Perspectives* 1(October):45-46.
Rivilin, Alice M.
  1972. Why can't we get things done? *Brookings Bulletin* 9(Spring):
         5-9.
Robinson, W. C., and Somboosuk, A.
  1969. Evaluating the economic benefits of fertility reduction.
         Studies in Family Planning 39(March):4-8.
Rogers, Everett M.
  1962. *Diffusion of innovations.* New York: Free Press.
  1969. *Modernization among peasants: The impact of communica-
         tion.* New York: Holt, Rinehart, and Winston.
Rogers, Everett M., and Shoemaker, F. Floyd.
  1971. *Communication of innovations: A cross-cultural approach.*
         New York: Free Press.
Rogers, Everett M., and Stanfield, J. David.
  1966. Adoption and diffusion of new products: Emerging gener-
         alizations and hypotheses. Paper presented at the Conference
         on the Application of Science to Marketing Management,
         Purdue University.
Rosen, B. C.
  1956. The achievement syndrome: A psychocultural dimension of
         social stratification. *American Sociological Review* 21(April):
         203-11.
  1959. The psychosocial origins of achievement motivation. *Sociom-
         etry* 22(September):203-11.
Ross, John.
  1966. United States: The Chicago fertility control studies. *Studies
         in Family Planning* 15(October):1-8.
Rotter, J. B.
  1966. Generalized expectancies for internal versus external control
         of reinforcement. *Psychological Monographs* 80:1-20.
Rotter, J. B., and Mulry, R. C.
  1967. Internal versus external control of reinforcement and deci-

REFERENCES   193

sion time. *Journal of Personality and Social Psychology* 2:598-604.

Ryder, Norman B., and Westoff, Charles F.
1967. The United States: The pill and the birth rate, 1960-1965. *Studies in Family Planning* 20(June):1-3.
1969. Relationships among intended, expected, desired, and ideal family size: United States, 1965. *Population Research* (March):1-7.

Schramm, Wilbur.
1964. *Mass media and national development.* Stanford: Stanford University Press.

Schwarzweller, Harry K., and Brown, James.
1969. Social structure of the contact situation: Rural Appalachia and urban America. Information Report no. 1. Morgantown: West Virginia University.

Sheppard, Harold L.
1967. *Effects of family planning on poverty in the United States.* Kalamazoo: W. E. Upjohn Institute for Employment Research.

Shryock, Henry S., Jr., and Larmon, Elizabeth A.
1965. Some longitudinal data on internal migration. *Demography* 2:579-92.

Shryock, Henry S., Jr., and Nam, Charles B.
1965. Educational selectivity of interregional migration. *Social Forces* 43(March):299-310.

Smith, David Horton, and Inkeles, Alex.
1966. The OM scale: A comparative socio-psychological measure of individual modernity. *Sociometry* 29(December):353-77.

Springer, Michael.
1970. Social indicators, reports and accounts: toward the management of society. *Annals of the American Academy of Political and Social Science* 388(March):1-13.

Stephens, Lowndes.
1970. Mass media exposure and modernization among the Appalachian poor. Paper presented to the Annuai Meeting of the Association for Education in Journalism, Theory and Methodology Division, Washington, D.C.

Stouffer, Samuel A.
1940. Intervening opportunities: A theory relating mobility and

distance. *American Sociological Review* 5(December): 845-67.

Stycos, J. Mayonne.
1970.   Public and private opinion on population and family planning. *Studies in Family Planning* 51(March):10-17.

Stycos, J. Mayonne, and Weller, Robert H.
1967.   Female working roles and fertility. *Demography* 4:210-17.

Suval, Elizabeth M., and Hamilton, C. Horace.
1965.   Some new evidence on educational selectivity in migration to and from the South. *Social Forces* 43(May):536-47.

Thurow, Lester C.
1969.   *Poverty and Discrimination.* Washington, D.C.: Brookings Institute.

Torgerson, W. S.
1958.   *Theory and methods of scaling.* New York: Wiley.

United States, Bureau of the Census.
1960.   *United States census of population.* Washington, D.C.: Department of Commerce.
1969.   Current Population Reports, series P-60, no. 68, Poverty in the United States—1959 to 1968. Washington, D.C.: Government Printing Office.
1970a. Current Population Reports, series P-20, no. 196, Changes in the average number of children ever born to women: 1960 to November 1969. Washington, D.C.: Government Printing Office.
1970b. Current Population Reports, series P-60, no. 75, Income in 1969 of families and persons in the United States. Washington, D.C.: Government Printing Office.
1970c. Current Population Reports, series P-60, no. 76, 24 million Americans—poverty in the United States: 1969. Washington, D.C.: Government Printing Office.
1971a. Current Population Reports, series P-20, no. 211, Previous and prospective fertility: 1967. Washington, D.C.: Government Printing Office.
1971b. Current Population Reports, series P-23, no. 36, Fertility indicators: 1970. Washington, D.C.: Government Printing Office.
1971c. Current Population Reports, series P-60, no.77, Poverty in-

creases by 1.2 million in 1970. Washington, D.C.: Government Printing Office.

1973. Current Population Reports, series P-60, no. 91, Characteristics of the low-income population: 1971. Washington, D.C.: Government Printing Office.

United States, Bureau of Labor Statistics.

1969. *Three standards of living for an urban family of four persons,* bulletin no. 1570-5 (March).

1970. *The consumer price index for October 1970.* Washington, D.C.: Government Printing Office.

United States, Department of Agriculture.

1965. *Consumer expenditure and income.* USDA Consumer Expenditure Survey report no. 20, Agricultural Research Service Public USDA. Washington, D.C.: Government Printing Office.

United States, Department of Health, Education, and Welfare.

1969. Differentials in health characteristics by color, United States July 1965-June 1967. *Vital Health Statistics,* series 10, no. 56 (October).

1970. *The health of children—1970.* Public Health Service. Washington, D.C.: Government Printing Office.

United States, Senate.

1970. *The national nutritional survey. Hearings before the Select Committee on Nutrition and Human Needs,* pt. 3(April 23).

Useem, John, and Donoghue, John and Ruth.

1963. Men in the middle of the third culture. *Human Organization* 22:169-79.

Veroff, J. A., Atkinson, J. W., Feld, Sheila C., and Gurin, G.

1960. The use of thematic apperception to assess motivation in a nationwide interview study. *Psychological Monographs* 74 no. 12 (whole no. 499).

Weber, Max.

1930. *The Protestant ethic and the spirit of capitalism.* Translated by T. Parsons. New York: Scribner.

Weller, Jack E.

1966. *Yesterday's people: Life in contemporary Appalachia.* Lexington: University of Kentucky Press.

Westley, Bruce H.
　1971.　Communication and social change. *American Behavorial Scientist* 14(May-June):719-43.
Westoff, C. F., and Ryder, N. B.
　1967.　United States: Methods of fertility control, 1955, 1960 & 1965. *Studies in Family Planning* 17(February):1-5.
Whelpton, P. K., Campbell, Arthur A., and Patterson, John E.
　1966.　*Fertility and family planning in the United States.* Princeton: Princeton University Press.
Whiting, Gordon C., and Stanfield, J. David.
　1972.　Mass media use and opportunity structure in rural Brazil. *Public Opinion Quarterly* 36 (Spring):56-68.
Widner, Ralph R.
　1970.　The region's economy shows gains. *Appalachia* 3 (February): 11-13.
Wilber, George L.
　1963.　Migration expectancy in the United States. *Journal of the American Statistical Association* (June):444-53.
　1968.　Fertility and the need for family planning among the rural poor in the United States. *Demography* 5:894-909.
　1972.　Systematic indicators of regional poverty. *Growth and Change* 3(July):11-15.
Williamson, J. B.
　1970.　Subjective efficacy and ideal family size as predictors of favorability toward birth control. *Demography* 7 (August): 329-39.
Winterbottom, Marian R.
　1958.　The relation of need for achievement to learning experiences in independence and mastery. In *Motives in fantasy, action, and society,* ed. J. W. Atkinson, pp. 45-78. New York: Van Nostrand.
Zetterberg, Hans L.
　1965.　*On theory and verification in sociology.* Totowa, N.J.: Bedminster Press.

Contributors

George L. Wilbur is the director of the Social Welfare Research Institute of the University of Kentucky.

Thomas E. Hammock is an assistant professor in the Department of Sociology of Grambling College.

Daniel E. Jaco is a research associate of the Social Welfare Research Institute of the University of Kentucky.

J. Patrick Madden is a professor in the Department of Agricultural Economics of Pennsylvania State University.

Philip C. Palmgreen is an assistant professor in the School of Communications of the University of Kentucky.

Thomas R. Panko is an assistant professor in the Department of Sociology of the University of Southern Mississippi.

Jon M. Shepard is an associate professor in the Department of Sociology of the University of Kentucky.

Martha M. Woods is a graduate student in the Department of Psychology of the University of Kentucky.